NEEDLEPAINTING

Other books by Bruce David Colen

MEET ME IN THE DOGHOUSE

Eszter Haraszty
and Bruce David Colen

NEEDLEPAINTING
A GARDEN OF STITCHES

Liveright New York

LIVERIGHT
500 Fifth Avenue
New York, New York 10036

1.98765432

Library of Congress Cataloging in Publication Data
Haraszty, Eszter.
Needlepainting, a garden of stitches.
1. Embroidery.   I. Colen, Bruce David, joint author.   II. Title.
TT770.H26   746.4′4   74-13423
ISBN 0-87140-593-8

Designed by Sandra Kandrac

In memory of my mother, Elizabeth—
  Who never thought I would mend my ways;
And my father, Michael—
  Who loved wild flowers.

Preface

We sew, sew, prick our fingers, dull our sight,
Producing what? . . . A cushion, where you lean
And sleep, and dream of something we are not,
But would be for your sake.
  —Elizabeth Barrett Browning: *Aurora Leigh,* 1857

Ms. Browning never met my wife, Eszter Haraszty.

Granted, the latter's fingers and face are usually sienna stained after laboring in the garden, but I have yet to notice any trickling blood at the conclusion of an embroidery session. On the matter of eyesight, I am the one who, having forgotten my glasses, must ask to have the menu read aloud like a child dining out. As to napping on the embroidered sofa? Of course I do, and often, upon awakening, I find that my wife has tucked in one of our dogs or cats to keep me company.

At those times, Ms. Browning, I never dream that my wife is something she is not—may Freud be my witness. Quite the contrary, my reveries sometimes concern how blissful it would be if she, and our home, stayed the way they were for a while. But that will never happen as long as flowers bloom in our garden, challenging her to find new ways to embody and celebrate their beauty. Floors have come up, ceilings down and walls changed to accommodate her flower designs in tiles, stained-glass skylights and wall fabric. I read under tulip- and buttercup-shaped lampshades, open a garage door on which there is a mural of four giant red poppies and sunbathe on a pool deck of hand-painted, abstract flowers. Her embroidery work has made our home a wall-to-wall garden, where the brilliant colors and fascinating designs of nature never wilt. I have yet to develop an allergy.

Originally, I had wanted my wife to call this book *An Embroidered Life*. Then I remembered that one Webster definition of "embroider" is "to embellish with fictitious details or exaggerations." The only thing which has been stretched in *Needlepainting, A Garden of Stitches* is the imagination of its creator, Eszter Haraszty.

BRUCE DAVID COLEN

April 1, 1974

Acknowledgments

Creative people are not the independent workers they often lead others to believe. Without help, critical appreciation and understanding, I would never have survived as a designer. Ivory towers are very cold and lonely places when there are no friendly visitors. I have been very fortunate that, over the years, so many kind and generous friends have paid calls—and returned mine.

Where to begin my thanks? In the United States, the best of starting places:

Marcel and Connie Breuer, who gave me courage in a strange land. The late Hans Knoll, the impresario of modern interior designers. He taught me what I could and should do. Charles Whitney and Olga Gueft (*Interiors*) and the late Lazette Gruen (Fairchild Publications) —the first to write about my fabric designs and use of color. Thanks must go to magazine and newspaper editors who believe in the taste of their readers: Shana Alexander (*McCall's*); Wallace Guenther and Marion Gough (*House Beautiful*); Ralph and Eleanor Graves (*Life*); Elizabeth Sverbeyeff (*House & Garden*); Frank Zachary (*Holiday* and

ix

Town & Country); James Toland, Carolyn Murray, and Mary Lou Luther (*The Los Angeles Times*); Wallace Carroll (*The New York Times*); and Harriet Morrison (*The New York Herald Tribune*).

Then there are the photographers: Herbert Matter, Gordon Parks, Hans Namuth, Dick Rutledge, Richard Gross and Howard Gordon, who fought too much sun, rain, darkness, smog and four curious cats to take the photographs for this book in eighteen days. The eye of the camera in the hands of an artist does more than record, it engrandizes. And my deep appreciation to the Awards Committee of the American Institute of Decorators and the foreign publications, *Domus* and *Maison & Jardin,* for honoring me as "an American Designer."

Without the enthusiasm and support of Mrs. Kelly Wallace, my type of embroidery might never have bloomed.

Finally, thank you, Bruce, for being my severest critic, my most enthusiastic audience. Who would have weeded "a garden of stitches" but you?

x

Contents

Introduction

It should become quickly evident to readers of *Needlepainting, A Garden of Stitches* that I am not an expert in the field of embroidery. But to avoid any possible confusion on this point, let me set the record straight.

Admirers of my work, seeing a piece of Needlepainting for the first time, frequently say, "But you're a professional. I could never do that. I don't have the talent."

However phrased, it is a cop-out. Talent is nine-tenths work, one-tenth inspiration. The former calls for discipline, the latter stems from an interest in something outside yourself. In my case, inspiration comes from the world of nature and flowers.

Am I a professional designer? Yes. A professional horticulturist? Maybe—I am working at it. A professional embroiderer? Definitely not. This country and these times are rich in women who have devoted life-long careers mastering the needle arts—accomplished experts like Erica Wilson, Elsa Williams and Jacqueline Enthoven. When it comes to being knowledgeable about embroidery techniques and the countless ways of stitching, I am an amateur in the company of these true professionals. Am I guilty of protesting too much? Hardly. Anyone who has heard me praise my own cooking knows that false modesty is certainly not a Haraszty trait.

I offer this disclaimer because in the chapters that follow you will be reading how to do my form of embroidery, Needlepainting. While on that personal level my teaching credentials are valid, it does not follow that more accomplished craftsmen may not know better, quicker or easier ways of doing the same things.

I feel strongly about design, color, flowers, animals—you name it —but I abhor giving advice or acting as an arbiter of taste. Those roles are directly opposed to what I believe in most: the freedom to express personally one's own creative self. So, while reading about my way of embroidering, remember: you don't necessarily have to do exactly as I say, or do as I do, but *do*.

It is the only way you will learn how good you are.

ESZTER HARASZTY

California
1974

1 Beginner's Luck

I had best say it right away: I always thought that any form of embroidery was a bore. I did, that is, until necessity and the chance discovery of a simple needlework technique, Needlepainting, made me change my mind.

The long-standing aversion to anything connected with a needle and thread goes back to my early school days in Hungary. Our teachers were no different than those of any other country in their insistence that every little girl had to learn sewing if she wanted to grow up to be a good woman. At six, I was not at all sure that I wished to become a woman, let alone a good one. It seemed to me that boys had much more fun in life. Besides, I hated the year-long monotony of making what was then called a "sampler ribbon"—thirty or so white linen squares, each of which had to be covered with a different stitch exercise. At the end of the school term, we sewed our completed squares together and backed the bell-pull-like strip with pink silk. For me, it was a talisman of torture.

The white linen was indelibly finger smudged, my sample stitches were as easy to identify as a single strand in a pot of spaghetti and the silk, covering the badly knotted back side of my embroidery, had a serious case of measles. To this day, during moments of doubt and inadequacy, my memory goes back to the humiliating evening when the students exhibited their samplers. Mine was hung in the darkest corner of the classroom, obscured from all but the curious eyes of my parents. To cover my embarrassment, I recall haughtily telling my mother, "Embroidery is a peasant hobby." For the following twenty years, the only time I picked up a needle was when a hem fell down. And that wasn't very often, since I discovered maintenance-free blue jeans the moment I discovered America in 1947. But, as I said, eventually pure and simple need turned that cursed instrument into a wondrous tool of self-expression.

The about-face took place at the beginning of the 1960s, when my husband and I bought an acre and a half of hilltop privacy in Los Angeles. The house which stood upon it was an afterthought—and looked it. The setting had been first in importance because, like most ex-New Yorkers, we were garden, tree and sun starved. Having remodeled other people's homes as part of my professional career, the idea of transforming our own was a satisfaction I looked forward to. It is now fourteen years later, we are still remodeling and the pleasures have not stopped, although it looked at times as though our bank account would.

Once the structural changes of our new house were finished, once the carpenters, masons, plumbers, electricians and painters had left, leaving their mess behind, I started the exciting part—planning the interiors. I wanted the house to have the airy, open feeling of California living. I visualized the place as looking as if we had invited the outdoors in to stay. That meant rooms of bright sunlit colors like the poppy beds and acacia trees encircling the house. This extension of

1. One day's harvest—a year's supply of Needlepainting subjects.

2. Color and yarn key for Oriental poppy sampler.

3. Step 1: having transferred design to linen, color center and leaf with felt-tipped pen.

4. Step 2: outline flower in chain stitches. Embroider colors 1 thru 4 and ink for yarn #5.

5. Step 3: pack red satin stitches against each other, like people on a rush-hour subway. Ink #6, #7.

6. Step 4: when using yarns #6 and #7, be sure to satin-stitch atop satin stitch for three-dimensional look.

7. Step 5: the best part. As you Needlepaint the final area, the Oriental poppy comes to life.

I.

3.

II.

4.

III.

5.

IV.

6.

V.

7.

8. The living room. You might call it the nursery, for here my first
Needlepaintings started to bloom and spread.

9.

9. Iceland poppies: the purest, the most brilliant, and translucent colors I've found in nature.

10. Circular-armed Thonet chair with poppy garland seat.

11. The Thonet lounge, my first Needlepainting project, was almost the last—it took over ten square feet of stitches.

10.

11.

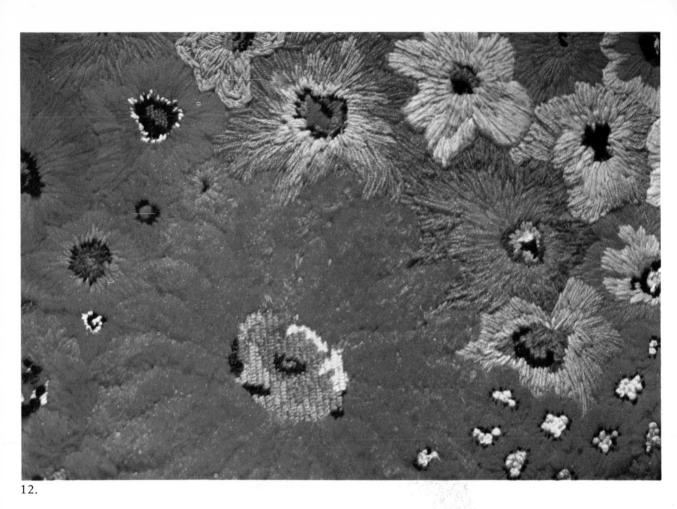

12.

13. . . . because of the thousands and thousands of tightly placed stitches.

12. Close-up of the Thonet lounge. It has survived fourteen years of wear . . .

13.

nature was particularly important in the living-room area, where two large skylights looked up at a 300-year-old California live oak and where a whole wall of French doors faced the gardens. We had an old Thonet chaise in this room, and it seemed only right that the piece should be covered in a flower design. However, none of the fabric stores had what I wanted. I explained the problem to my husband. "They all look like flower prints."

"Isn't that what you were looking for?"

"Yes, but I'm after a fabric that *suggests* a field of flowers. All the designs come complete with thorns, leaf veins and Latin names. There was even one with flecks of pollen. The clerk sneezed when he showed it to me."

Then my husband said what he has a bad habit of saying: "Why don't you make something?"

His total faith in my creative abilities is wonderful—and infuriating. It reminds me of those people who assume that if you have lived in a particular place you are familiar with every one of its inhabitants. "Oh, you come from Budapest [population: 1,900,000], Miss Haraszty. You must know Laslo Zsoandzso." When you say no, they start on a head-to-toe description of the unknown person, thinking that will jog your memory. But Bruce was not as persistent. When I told him I did not know how to embroider, he dropped the matter—and the corners of his mouth.

The time had finally come to try and put aside childhood memories of needlework fiascos. Secretly, I bought some yarn and canvas. Then, behind the locked door of my studio, I struggled to teach myself crewel work. Having a block about instruction sheets, finding them as complicated and confusing as a government tax form, my first embroidery experiments were very scrambled. They went into a bottom drawer for none to see, especially myself.

The scruffy samples remained hidden until a good friend, Shana Alexander, dropped by one Sunday afternoon and asked: "What are you working on these days?"

"I'll show you what I am not working on." My adult version of a sampler ribbon was retrieved from the bottom drawer.

In a half-hour briefing before the fireplace, Shana retaught me three basic stitches: satin, chain and the French knot. (I have since enlarged my total repertoire to four by adding the turkey knot.) Years of foolish inhibitions dissolved during the thirty-minute refresher course, and, as soon as Shana left, I began to work out an embroidery design for that bentwood chaise. Indicative of my enthusiasm—and proof that ignorance is bliss—I should mention that the linen for this first needlework project was six feet long and twenty inches in width.

I think of myself as a Designer by profession, an Embroiderer by chance and an incurable Gardener by compulsion. With such a triadic personality, it is not surprising that my initial embroidery design, and 98 percent of those that followed, incorporated flowers.

I truly love my garden. It satisfies a very basic need to be close to the soil, helping and watching things grow. I am drawn to nature —and nature draws me out—because it offers the purest forms of beauty and the truest colors. What greater pleasure, for one who needs flowers in her life, than to be able to grow and harvest her own?

Of course, California made such self-gratification relatively easy, but the inspiration and satisfaction of coexisting with plant life can be achieved even in a city. Before I was married, I did just that in a New York studio apartment. There must have been fifty different plants about the place, keeping me company, helping me forget the noise, soot and chill of urban living. Each morning, before getting down to work, I would make a tour of inspection, just as I now go garden-watching with my second cup of morning coffee. Picking off dead leaves and poking a finger in the soil to test the moisture content, you might say I was watching over them as well.

No indoor garden, especially in winter, can be very rich in color, and small miracles should be cherished. I remember one bleak February experimenting with lilies of the valley. Filling a long, shallow galvanized tray with Super Soil and Vermiculite, I planted a dozen or so pips at two-week intervals. Just as the first snowy white batch came into full bloom, a long-awaited assignment in Montego Bay materialized. A wonderful way to escape a New York winter, yet leaving those lilies of the valley alone in an empty apartment bothered me very much. While I was away, a friend would be running in to water my garden, but nobody would be really enjoying the brave, bright wonder of those small lilies. The gentleman who was driving me to the airport was Mrs. Eleanor Roosevelt's physician, and he agreed to give the abandoned lilies to her for permanent adoption. While he toted my luggage to the car, I carried the tray of delicate flowers. It was a freezing, windy morning. In the twenty-odd steps from front door to car door, the plants froze. When I put the tray down on the back seat of the car, one by one the fragile flowers made a drooping arch and died. Even in death, their lovely fragrance filled the car. Seeing the tears in my eyes, no one would have suspected that I was about to escape to a tropical island for a working vacation. Every day for the four weeks I was in Jamaica, I thought of those lilies of the valley. How stupid of me not to have known that these artificially forced bulbs needed artificial heat conditions to keep them alive. I swore to myself then that if I were ever fortunate enough to live in the country and have a garden of my own, I would never plant a bulb, seedling, plant, bush or tree until I had studied and learned its habits and needs. I've kept that promise, thanks to loquacious nurserymen, gardening magazines and an ever-growing shelf of books on horticulture.

My yearning to be surrounded by flowers in a winter apartment became common knowledge. Gentlemen callers were pleased to learn that I much preferred receiving a big bouquet of flowers to an expensive dinner—not that I would have turned down both. And when I was alone and finances were tight, I usually bypassed the butcher on my way to the flower stalls in the old Washington Market. Spring, summer and fall were much easier, but harder on my friends who thoughtfully invited me for weekends at their houses in the country. When they woke up Monday mornings they would see me judiciously —careful not to leave too many barren spots—plundering their gardens. When it was time to drive back to town, I would be sitting in the rear seat surrounded by buckets and baskets of loot. Depending on the season, my hosts would find me barricaded behind pussy willow, forsythia, or peach and cherry branches which just needed a little forcing to burst into bloom. Later in the year there were wild flowers and black-eyed Susans, followed by pickings from the summer gardens and walks in the farm fields for sheaves of rye and wheat. Then, as the visiting-growing season drew to a close, I concluded my foraging with big bundles of fall leaves.

I remember one August Monday getting up before anyone else so that I might spend half an hour in the Wolfes' lower marshland searching for some very special ferns. By the time I returned to the house with a pailful of these delicate green fronds, Bob had given up and driven off. It was ten o'clock.

With this background of floramania, one can guess how quickly I went overboard, fathoms beyond my depth, when we bought those tillable acres in Southern California. I spent our first year as land-owners working from morning to dusk, planting the flowers, bushes and trees I had always dreamed of caring for: marguerites, shasta daisies, lupine, larkspur, white sweet peas, anemones, ranunculus, cyclamen, old-fashioned roses, acacia trees and flowering fruits and on and

6

on. I have paid a price for that year-long binge—thirteen years of constant labor to maintain what I sowed so generously. However, that is one debt I will be happy never to stop repaying.

In that initial harvest, I saw my first Iceland poppy outside the pages of botanical books or on picture postcards from teasing friends in California. My standards for beauty and color would never be the same again. Actually, the discovery was almost put off to the next growing season because of another West Coast specialty—the omnivorous snail. My initial one hundred poppy settings—now I plant eight times that number each October—took flight before they took root. Each morning, when I went out to check their progress, a dozen or so of the tender shoots had disappeared. Getting down on my hands and knees, like someone searching for a contact lens, I found that the plants had been decapitated at soil level. I telephoned our local plant doctor, the nursery owner, and related "The Case of the Purloined Poppies." As a gardener-in-training, I was making so many similar distress calls that Jim Stevens did not have to ask who was on the phone before starting his diagnosis. "Some deer must have gotten into your garden, Eszter."

"The whole place is surrounded by an eight-foot fence."

"Well, then, what about rabbits?"

"You're forgetting our two Great Danes."

"How about gophers?"

"Bruce set so many traps in that area, he calls it The Mine Field."

"Field mice?"

"Four cats."

"What about those chickens you've got up there?"

"They're locked up in the henhouse at night."

"What about Brinks?" Jim was referring to our pet raccoon.

"He's only interested in the chickens."

"Then it's got to be snails, Eszter."

"But I haven't seen any. Come by and look for yourself."

"That's because they eat at night and sleep it off during the day, hidden under some cool leaf."

Instead of making a house call, Dr. Stevens sent up a 25-pound bag of snail pellets. The poppy thieves ate themselves into a permanent stupor, and I was able to watch the remaining thirty plants reach maturity. Seeing my first Iceland poppy struggle out of its green straitjacket, freeing crinkled, tissue-paper petals to the sun, was somehow a reaffirmation of so many important things: courage, hope, beauty and life itself.

They come to bloom in February and that is when I begin my routine of morning harvests, after the animals have been fed but before my own breakfast. It is one of my favorite moments of the day, seeing the sun highlight this fantastic riot of pure, singing colors. I pick each flower and those buds where the color is beginning to show. With the bundle of brilliant reds, yellows, oranges and pinks in my arms, I head for the combination doghouse–potting shed where we have a gas burner. By charring the ends of the poppies, sealing their gum-filled stems full of moisture, they last longer as cut flowers. This lovely way to start a day goes on until about the Fourth of July, when the poppies succumb to the summer heat. Until the following February, they live on in my memory and work.

As the Iceland poppy grew to be the hallmark of our garden, it also became the trademark of my output as a designer. I have used their simple, bold shapes in stained-glass windows, in fabric and wallpaper designs and as the pattern for ceramic floor tiles. When a label and signature lining was needed for my first—and last—fashion collection, it was the Iceland poppy. I have made lampshades in their image and used their likeness on table umbrellas. For special parties, I have painted poppies on tablecloths, napkins and place cards. At one very special occasion, they just happened to show up on my toenails.

The questionable distinction of being known as the Poppy Lady is clearly of my own making. My husband and our friends find the association doubly amusing. They claim that, because of my Hungarian accent, whenever I mention the flower they look around for little dogs. The confusion takes place because they *hear* with an American accent.

While the ubiquitous Iceland poppy appears in so many of my embroidery pieces, it is absent from the cover for the Thonet chaise (see plate 11); although, as I look at the photograph myself, it seems a few Flanders poppies—every spring their blazing color made the Hungarian *puszta* look as though somebody had set a series of small brush fires—subconsciously slipped into the design. What I was really after was the blending of colors and shapes one associates with a field of wild flowers. We had just such a natural vista down by the gate, a miniature meadow carpeted with native flora and marguerites. I remember walking down there with Dorka and Iago, the Great Danes, on the afternoon of Shana's tutoring session. As the dogs played hide-and-seek among the chest-high daisy bushes, I gathered a basketful of flowers, a sampling of what the meadow looked and smelled like in spirit, if not in blossom-for-blossom fact.

With a vaseful of these pickings on my drawing table for reference and encouragement, I started to work out an allover design, using a sheet of tracing paper cut to match the size of the linen. Being really quite bad at sketching freehand, I felt no compulsion about lifting a particular blossom out of the vase and holding it an inch above the drawing, so that I might better approximate its shape and study the convoluted center. A day and two erasers later I was as close to what I wanted as I would ever get. The design was transferred to the white linen, using sheets of carbon paper. Then, I did what I never did again—colored in the entire pattern with tempera. An obvious ploy to put off the moment of embroidering. For another week, the canvas lay stretched over the chaise while I debated if it was right. My husband was no help. He said it was.

I had stalled long enough. It was time to thread my needle and start.

2 The Four Stitches

While only a novice would have been foolish enough to select a ten-square-foot piece of embroidery as a beginning project, there were certain advantages in starting too big. First, every undertaking thereafter seemed like child's play. Second, I had a big canvas, so to speak, on which to experiment, make mistakes and learn. And, third, when the cushion for the chaise was finally completed—it took nearly six months of after-dinner homework—the finished piece turned out to be so visually exciting, so personally gratifying, I was inspired to go on embroidering until the whole living room basked in sunshine and flowers. (See plate 8.) I might not have felt so committed had my first needlework piece been a quiet little pillow.

A work pattern was set up during those first six months which has rarely been altered. My days were booked from nine to five, keeping one step ahead of the garden's seasonal demands and staying even with my design assignments. (The race to keep up with household duties had been lost the moment it started.) Needlework became an evening affair, except when I had a take-the-day-off cold or some magazine wanted a picture story "on how you really work" but "we have to photograph in daylight."

I quickly discovered that, while enjoying the end result of needlework, the act itself, when pursued for any length of time, became tedious. Some sort of distraction was needed from the repetitious work, but one that required little attention, since my primary concentration had to be on stitches and color. My husband's work, television, provided the perfect take-it-or-leave-it relief. Bruce worked all day at Metro-Goldwyn-Mayer supervising the various television series, which meant seeing the film over and over again until it was broadcast-ready. Came evening, he simply could not face one more "Dr. Kildare" operation or a domestic crisis in "Please Don't Eat the Daisies"; although, "Someone ought to watch if the network ran the reels in the right order." The honor fell to me. Since those days, I have done my embroidery on the study couch, *listening* to mystery shows and old movies as an antidote to monotony. "M*A*S*H," "Maude" and "All in the Family," on the other hand, are not good programs to embroider by. Those I want to *watch*.

When Shana Alexander became editor of *McCall's,* she asked her ex-pupil to create some embroidery kits for the magazine's readers. In the same issue which offered the designs, there was to be an article on Eszter Haraszty needlework. It needed a title. I chose "Needlepainting," since that combination of words best describes both the technique and end result of my sort of embroidery. Like painting a flower, you cover a canvas with layer upon layer of pigment. In this case, the pigment is yarn; the canvas is linen. And, as with an oil painting, the finished work has depth and texture. (See plate 7.)

Today, if a guest looks at my embroidery and says, "Oh, I could never do that, it's much too hard," I remind them that the effect has been achieved with four, just four, simple stitches.

Starting with the chain stitch, I outline the entire design which

12

has been transferred to linen. (See figures 1a, 1b, and 1c.) Not only does this allow one to see the pattern in toto, but by using yarn as a guide, instead of relying on an inked or painted border, you avoid the possibility of smearing the markings with moist fingers.

Beginners, wanting to practice the chain stitch, might care to do what I did to perfect that technique. I made embroidered animal crackers. (See figure 2.) The shapes were actually copied from a batch of Christmas cookies I once designed. Each silhouette is cut out from felt and filled in with row upon row of nothing but chain stitches. The likenesses are not very good, but the masked one always makes me smile. That was Brinks, the pet raccoon who stole his way into our larder, bed and hearts.

I usually begin to embroider from the darker, inner part of each flower outward toward the lighter shaded periphery. Perhaps I follow this course because that is the way flowers seem to unfold in nature; but one thing is certain, saving the more delicate whites, pinks and yellows to the end cuts down on the amount of washing which usually has to be done when the embroidery is finished. (Also, the actual center, the heart of each flower, is a pain in the neck to do, so I get each of them over with as soon as possible.)

By using different sizes of satin stitches, the interwoven darks and lights are threaded into the chain-stitch border. (See figures 3a and 3b.) As you do this, use your thumb or needle to push aside the yarn so that extra stitches can be packed into an area. Also, if strands are pulled so tight that they form a straight line, you lose the undulating appearance of petals. I push and pull constantly, sculpting and coaxing the yarn into lifelike shapes.

No thread-thrifty person will ever turn out a first-rate Needle-painting. You have to have a touch of the extravagant in your soul to build up those layers upon layers of yarn until the petals and leaves of each flower become tiny, lush cushions. Thread your needle with

13

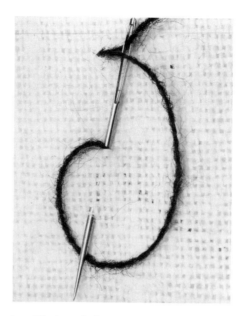

1a. Chain stitch.

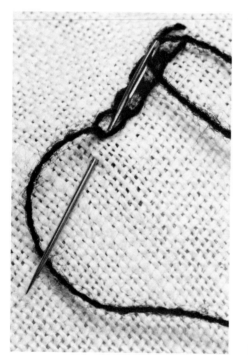

1b. Chain stitch.

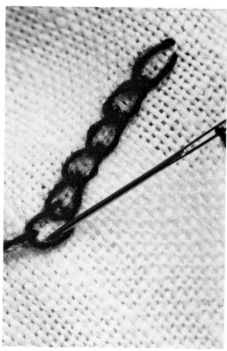

1c. Chain stitch.

2. An exercise in chain stitch.

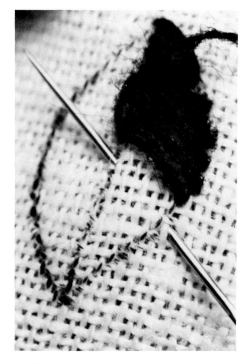

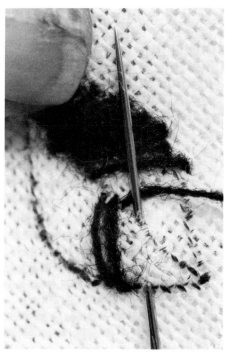

3a. Satin stitch.

3b. Satin stitch.

double, triple, sometimes quadruple strands of yarn. That is when coaxing becomes pushing, but it is the only way you can build up the textured, three-dimensional effect.

If you will forgive a shameful pun, it is the turkey knot which really gobbles up yarn. (See figures 4a, 4b, 4c, 4d, and 4e.) I use it to approximate the bulbous, seed-carrying centers of many flowers, particularly daisies, poppies and sunflowers. Having stitched in a solid bunch of yarn loops, I use my scissors to prune the cluster into a convex crown, rather like giving a crew haircut. I also used sheared turkey knots to make What-a-Puss's cheeks so bushy. (See plate 52.)

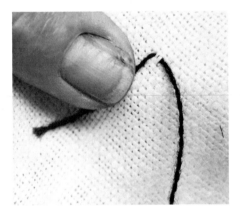

4a. Turkey knot.

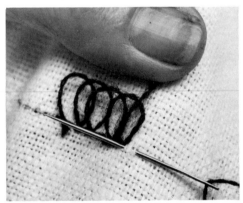

4b. Turkey knot.

4c. Turkey knot.

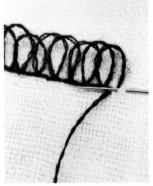

4d. Turkey knot.

4e. Turkey knot.

16

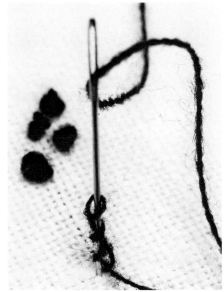

5a. French knot.   5b. French knot.

The French knot, like the French, is less profligate. (See figures 5a and 5b.) And I use it sparingly, mostly to show pollen-bearing stamens. Sometimes there will be a group of French knots clustered in the center of a flower to indicate a pistil which is more delicately constructed than the ones which call for turkey knots.

There are my four stitches. Certainly it is a slim bag of tricks and one which no embroiderer need be afraid of mastering, especially beginners. But if those who would like to try Needlepainting need further inducement, let me add that this is one type of needlework where mistakes are hidden. Actually, they can be made to work for you. Never pull out a stitch that has gone askew—embroider over it. If you have a short piece of thread left in your needle, don't cut it off. Use it up. Accuracy is all very well for scientists, but when an embroiderer thinks only of being technically proficient, her work becomes a cold, precise exercise—and looks it. As in nature, irregularity is beautiful. (See plate 55.)

17

The very nonrealistic nature of Needlepainting gives the novice embroiderer additional room to err. After all, if a beginner wants to do a pillow covered with wild strawberries, her work need not look real enough to eat. The colors used, the sense of balance and freedom, the feeling of dimension—the total impression—are far more important than whether the strawberries have fuzz or if the leaves contain the correct number of veins. No botanist, worthy of his degree, would give me passing grades for the accuracy of my poppy designs, but that is what those marvelous flowers look and feel like to me. And, so far, no one has confused them with tulips or roses. For photographic exactness, turn in your yarn and linen for a camera.

My favorite story about never knowing what you can achieve unless you try concerns my husband's daughter. When Betsy was six or seven, she spent part of the summer at a day camp on Long Island. One of her counselors suggested she try painting.

Betsy said, "I can't."

"Well, what about making something with clay?"

"I can't."

The counselor was young and not about to give up. The next day, right after lunch, she took her charge down to the beach.

"Now, Betsy, here's a piece of beaver board and a bottle of glue. Walk along the beach, pick up anything you want and stick it to the board. You can do that, can't you?"

Faced with the alternative of going back to camp for a nap, Betsy turned beachcomber and collected shells, stones, bits of wood and sand. An hour later she had collaged a portrait of a little girl, hands on hips, who you would swear was saying, "I can't." That portrait now hangs in an honored spot on our living-room wall. Serious art collectors, even one museum curator, have looked at it and said, "What a great Klee."

My exhortations to be overly generous in the use of yarn are not

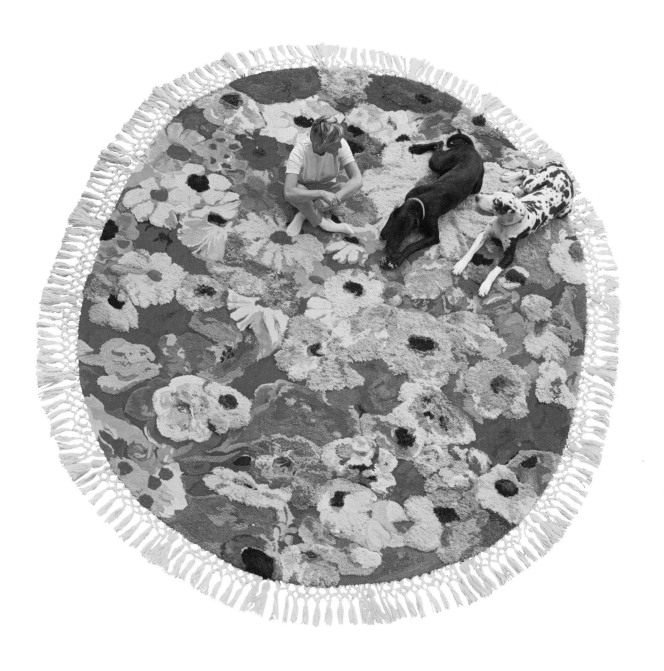

14. My first design commission in California reflects my wonderment
at the profuse, bright flowers I saw blanketing the countryside.

15. Another version of the garland design adapted for six dining chairs and a hooked rug.

16. California poppies cover the seat of a gift which came all the way from an attic in Finland.

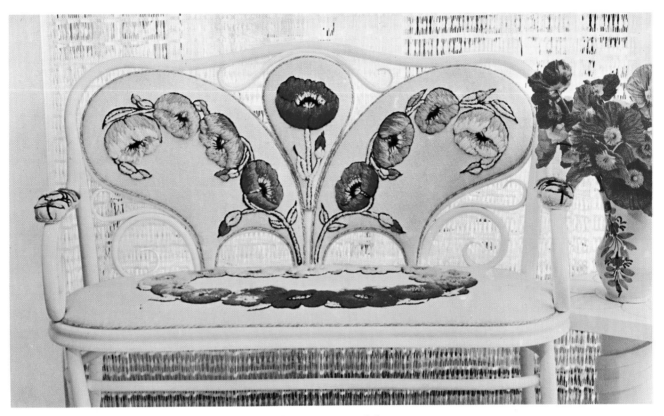

17. The most delicate of the bentwood pieces, the settee, called for a simple, airy design.

18. A spray of Iceland poppies on the seat graduates in color as it follows the curve of the settee's back.

19.

20.

19. A smaller field of flowers, an outgrowth of the chaise cover, was used for the popular Thonet rocker.

20. Closer view of the seat cushion. The sunflower's turkey knot center rises $3/8$ of an inch above the petals.

21. All the living-room furniture was lacquered white to frame the Needlepaintings unobtrusively.

22. A close-up, showing how small and large flowers are bunched together to make an embroidered fabric.

21.

22.

23. A flower of flowers. What was supposed to be a small draft screen grew to wall-hanging proportions.

24. Does embroidery mix with contemporary? To find out, I Needlepainted these classic chairs designed by Marcel Breuer.

23.

24.

25. Also, taking liberties with nature, a trellis of Iceland poppies started climbing across the seat . . .

26. . . . and, then, up the back of each chair. The flowers cushion what once was wicker.

25.

26.

27. For me, needlepoint does not have the same depth or lushness found in expanses of Needlepainting.

28. This one flower, like many of its neighbors, was embroidered with just two stitches: satin and French knots.

27.

28.

merely for aesthetic reasons. There is a practical advantage, too. The more layers you build up, the longer your finished work will survive. Those sandwiched stitches are a form of insurance against wear and tear. If the surface level goes, there are still four or five layers left. For me, to be worth doing, embroidery must have a utilitarian value. It should be used and enjoyed in one's daily life, not simply hung on a wall as a look-what-I-did trophy. That is why so many pieces in our house have been upholstered with, or fashioned from, Needlepainting. I have yet to see any worn spots on the first seat coverings, pieces which are a dozen years old. Occasionally, I have to snip off a loose or broken thread, but nobody is the wiser unless it is the birds. Each spring I throw outdoors my collection of yarn ends, bits and pieces too short for embroidery. The blue jays pick up the remnants and weave them into their nests. The latter end up looking like tiny, gaily colored Easter baskets. Too bad beer cans are not recycled that beautifully.

Nor should any reader think that my Needlepainted fabrics have lasted this long because the house is treated with "Please Do Not Touch" reverence. There are no velvet ropes tied across chair seats. In fact, when it comes to sitting down a lot, my husband need stand for no one. As for our not having to worry about the messy ways of children, we have literally lived with three Great Danes, one German shepherd, one pregnant golden retriever, a raccoon and six shedding cats who were in full possession of all their claws. If that menagerie could be taught not to touch, scratch or soil, children can too.

As for adults? There is something about beauty which engenders respect. Two years ago, 140 members of the Southern California Embroiderers Guild toured the house. The morning of their arrival the radio announced, "There is a ten-percent possibility of showers in the Los Angeles Basin today." I looked out the window—our front walk was 100 percent covered with two inches of muddy rainwater. Before I got to the front hall with a stack of mop-up towels, the first visitor, in stocking feet, was touring the house. She had left her shoes outside the door. One hundred and thirty-nine other women did the same. The front steps could have been taken for the shoe-blocked entrance to a Japanese temple. The house was so immaculate when the guild members left, two hours later, I still think they must have smuggled in a professional cleaning crew, while I worked in my studio.

Going back to the pluses of Needlepainting, I must mention what some may think is a minus. It is exercise. When you start working in the third or fourth stratum of two- or three-stranded yarn, your fingers, wrist, elbow and shoulder let you know they would rather be playing bridge. Of course the strain of pushing and pulling can be diminished to a ladylike level if one uses an embroidery hoop. But for me that is like making bread by placing a frozen piece of store-bought dough in the oven. My fingers only ache if they do not know what they are doing. They must be free to feel the tension of the fabric as it stretches and is pulled by the draw of the stitches. It takes time and testing to learn how loose or tight each thread should be. Practice is the sole answer.

3 From Start to Finishing

While I prefer to draw my embroidery concepts freehand, I know, and appreciate, that it is an impossibility for many. At least they think it is and the block is there. Until one gets up enough courage to try sketching a design of her own, or if that moment never comes, there is absolutely nothing wrong with outright copying.

Those with the urge to try embroidery should think of themselves as students, and beginners learn the fundamentals of any art by modeling their work after the masters. Under these circumstances, copying a favorite's print or drawing is truly the sincerest form of flattery. If the thought of using a piece of carbon paper still bothers you, remember Needlepainting is a very inexact technique. By the time you have pulled through the last stitch, your own personality will have shaped and changed the design so it will bear little resemblance to the original. One large sheet of carbon paper is all that stands between needleworkers and the satisfaction of making something from start to finish. And there is a special pride in knowing that what you are embroidering is unique, not a mass-produced pattern which ten or fifty thousand other women across the country are working on.

An old flower print hidden away in an attic box, a torn-out ad for floral sheets, the photo of a family pet, the illustration on a seed packet, a favorite still life in an art folio—anything that has special meaning for you can be transferred to a piece of white linen.

FINDING A FLOWER YOU LIKE

There are probably more source books for studying and duplicating flower designs than any other category. About ten years ago, I found my favorites in a bookshop in Copenhagen. They were three little volumes by Eigil Kiaer, filled from cover to cover with marvelous watercolor drawings of wild flowers, annuals and bulbs, perennials and water plants. Fortunately, in 1971 Macmillan brought out the series in this country, using the original Danish color plates. They are inexpensive and invaluable for anyone who does not have the good fortune to study flowers face to face. I crib from them myself when a drawing of a particular blossom does not seem right and the real thing is not growing in the garden at that moment. Two other volumes that contain superb—in color and accuracy of detail—botanical drawings are *Flowers of the World,* by Frances Perry (Crown, 1972), and *Wild Flowers of the World,* by Brian D. Morley (Putnam, 1970).

By now, both books are probably on the "40% off" table of your bookstore. That is where I found mine and similar research treasures. But for 100-percent discounts, local libraries usually have several shelves devoted to illustrated botanical works. Then there are the free seed and plant catalogs from firms such as Burpee or organizations like The Netherlands Flower-Bulb Institute. Last, and least in size, next time you receive a letter from abroad be sure to notice the postmark. Europeans have a penchant for floral stamps. Do not let their minuscule size bother you. Any clearly defined design, no matter how small, can be enlarged.

There are various pentograph-type devices for sale at art supply stores which enable one to make bigger or smaller copies of a given drawing. However, for me at least, these Rube Goldberg contraptions have a split personality, both of which are beyond my comprehension. Acknowledging my lack of mechanical dexterity, I take the easy way —the route to our local blueprint shop. There, any drawing, photograph or page from a book can be made to fit the size of the planned Needle-painting. Of course, I pay for my ignorance. The larger the blowup, the bigger the bill.

LIFTING THE DESIGN

Having selected the flower or flowers you wish to duplicate in a Needle-painting, they must now be transferred to tracing paper. The latter may be bought in various sheet sizes and by the roll at all art supply stores and some stationers. It is worth spending a few extra pennies for heavy stock which will not tear apart under the pressure of a firmly applied pencil.

Place the tracing paper over the selected subject matter. (See figure 6.) Since the transparent sheets have an infuriating way of showing their independence by slipping this way and that, station some sort of heavy object at the four corners of the paper. I use dress cutter's weights, but any hefty thing will do—a meat pounder from the kitchen, a flatiron or wine bottles filled with sand.

Taking a #2 pencil, trace the principal lines of the picture you wish to incorporate in your design. On flowers, be sure to get the outer edge of the bloom, the separation of petals, the formation of the centers, the stems and the leaves. Copy shadowed areas with hatch marks for future reference.

Sometimes the lines of a drawing are so faint that it is difficult

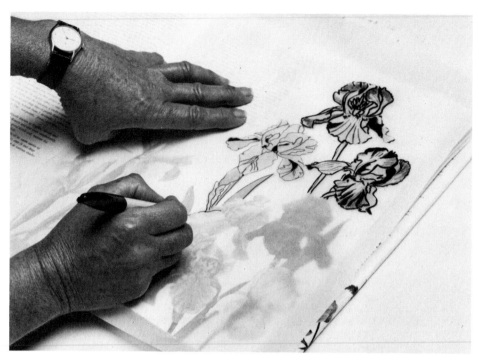

6. Tracing design from a book.

to see them through the tracing paper. When that happens to me, I go over them lightly with a soft lead pencil. My husband, a biblio-maniac, thinks this a capital crime. My public defense: books were meant to be used. Privately, as soon as the tracing is completed, I carefully erase the lines and some of my guilt.

FROM PAPER TO LINEN

Belgian linen is by far the best fabric for Needlepainting. It is an easy, durable texture to work with—porous enough to accommodate all the stitches required, yet sufficiently strong to weather the constant needle poking. I purchase the linen which comes closest to pure white. You will find it at needlecraft shops in 52-inch widths. Most stores are willing to split the bolt down to pieces 36 inches wide. Like every-

24

thing else these days, there is a shortage of quality linen, so do not be surprised if the price is high. Actually, the outlay for fabric is easier to take when you consider that most needlework projects call for much less than a yard of material.

If your needlecraft source does not have the linen you want, try fabric stores, remnant outlets or upholstery supply houses. Should you prefer a color or texture other than white linen, just be sure that the fabric is basket weave, often called evenweave. As the latter term implies, the warp and woof threads are the same size; and, in both directions, the threads are the same distance apart. You may be able to save a shopping trip by going through your box of odds and ends. The seats for the six dining chairs (see plate 15) were Needlepainted on different pieces of leftover woolen yardage which I found in the storage room. Be certain, also, that the basket weave you choose is substantial enough to hold up, and together, under the stress of embroidery.

Back to the copying process. Place your linen on a flat, smooth surface and over it put the sheet of tracing paper containing the penciled design. Insert between the two a sheet of good quality carbon paper, ink side against the linen. Art supply stores sell an 11-inch by 26-inch graphite paper, called dressmaker's carbon, but if you cannot locate this size, regular 8½-inch by 11-inch letter-size carbon paper will do. Should your design be bigger than the carbon paper you have, place two or more sheets side by side and see that they overlap a quarter inch or so to guarantee that no blanks show up on the imprinted linen. Again, weigh down the corners. (I once tried using our Persian cat as a paperweight. She stayed put but her tail didn't. I kept having to search through a silver gray boa to find my pencil marks.)

Now that the three layers are securely in place, take a sharp pencil and go over each line on your tracing-paper drawing. (See figure 7.) Press down firmly on the pencil, but not so heavily that the tracing tears apart. Your pencil will cut through the paper, though, along the

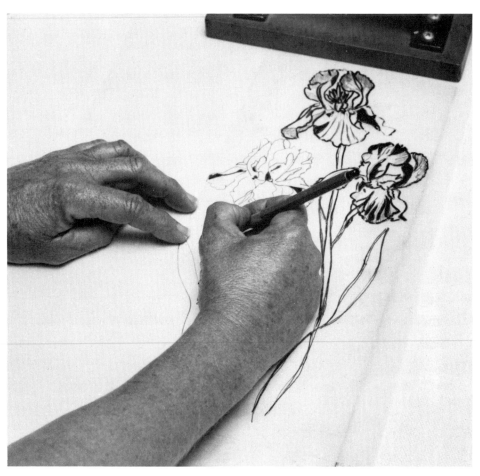

7. With carbon paper in place, push hard enough to mark linen.

line being traced. Stop every once in a while, carefully lift back the top sheet, and check if the imprint is coming through on the linen and that you are going over every line in the drawing. Keep your pencil sharp. I prefer honing mine on the little pads of fine sandpaper sold in art supply shops for this purpose. (See figure 8.) Once the design has been copied on linen, be sure to throw away the used carbon paper. If you save it for another time, your next transfer will be faded and hard to follow.

Save the tracing-paper drawing. You are about to fill in that de-

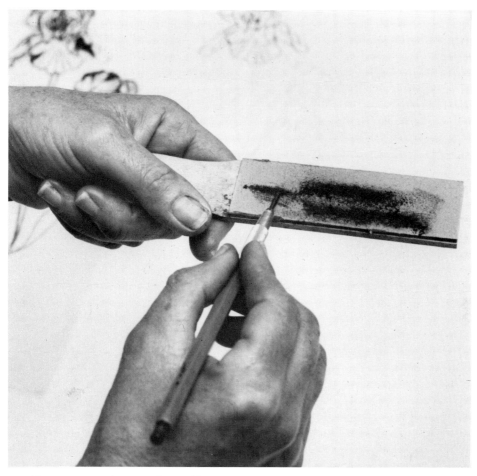

8. Always use a sharpened pencil.

sign with the various colors of the planned Needlepainting. One need not find an ink pen which perfectly matches the shades of wool you have in mind. The coloring is just a reference key. Magic Marker makes a broad felt, indelible pen which I favor, but there is no reason why colored pencils would not do. If you have second thoughts about how the design looks, now is the time to make revisions on the tracing-paper version. Keep the latter in your yarn basket as a reminder that, while embroidering, you want to make certain changes in line or shadow areas.

MARKING THE LINEN

Take your piece of linen and go over the carbon-papered lines with a black Magic Marker. (See figure 9.) This time use their fine-line pen. The precision point enables one to follow wriggly lines and sharp angles. Use a light hand, trying not to remember that the pen you are using contains indelible ink. It has to, or the design will eventually run, discoloring the linen and the light-shaded yarns. Actually, if you do make a slip while inking over the lines, it is not a tragedy. Irregularity, as I've said, is a blessed virtue in Needlepainting. Circumference lines or any other dividing borders, those calling for chain stitches, should be inked to a double thickness on the linen.

This emphasis on having a well-marked canvas undoubtedly goes back to my first efforts at needlework. I would be right in the middle of an embroidery session, going full swing and having fun, when I had to stop, squint and figure out vague pattern lines. My rhythm was broken, the pleasure ebbed. By the time I found my place, I wanted to call it quits for the night. I have seen the same faint, confusing linen designs on commercial embroidery kits. I asked a leading kit manufacturer why he didn't use darker lines. His answer: "Because needleworkers complain that they cannot hide heavy lines." That's silly. Instead of stitching up to the border, one simply embroiders just over it.

For the remainder of this chapter, the step-by-step instructions for making a Needlepainting have been correlated with see-for-yourself illustrations. (See plates 2–7.) Keep referring to this "how-to-do-it" sampler for visual help. My embroidered lines are clearer than my written ones.

I chose an Oriental poppy as the demonstration flower because the strong black accents in this bloom make the essential structure of the flower easier to perceive and to re-create with needle and yarn. Executing this Oriental poppy may prove a little complicated for the novice

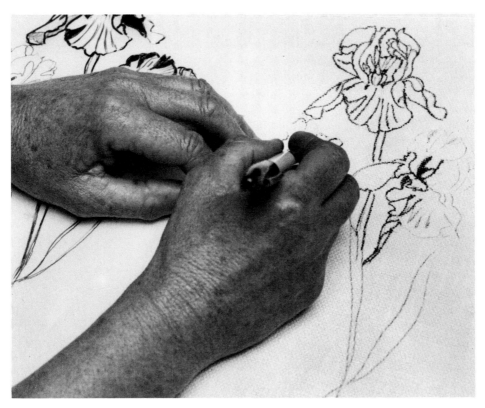

9. Ink over carbon lines on linen.

embroiderer. It was meant to be. So often, one is asked to master a simple exercise, only to find that the next step is mind-boggling. I think most women share my annoyance at being treated like backward beginners. There has to be a challenge to sustain interest, to provide a sense of accomplishment. And there is a private reward if you master this Oriental poppy—the knowledge that you are no longer a beginner in the art of Needlepainting. Good luck.

You will notice that each of my poppy petals is broken up into numerous fine-lined segments. I made these first on the tracing-paper drawing. Let me explain why, and what they stand for.

People are in the habit of saying, "A red rose" or "A yellow tulip." We label each blossom under one color, yet in nature there is no such thing. Look closely at what is called a red poppy and you will see that it is a bouquet of six, eight—sometimes a dozen—different reds. These variations in the petal pigment are multiplied and magnified by the play of sunlight and shadows. It is this shifting, luminous quality which I want to reflect in my flower designs. The only way I know how to do it is to play shade against shade, bounce one red off another. The human eye does the rest. It not only sees the highlights but, at the same time, synthesizes the contrasts and imagines the hues in between, the shades too numerous to duplicate in yarn. Those veinlike separations, drawn on the face of the petals, are my blueprint for this process of laying color against color.

With the paper work finished, so to speak, you may now get down to the real business of Needlepainting. For that, gather all your embroidering needs together in one basket. Mine contains the following:

1. The colored-in, tracing-paper design. You will be referring to it repeatedly.

2. All the yarns for the project at hand. (See Chapter 4 for various types and quality used.)

3. A small, fine-pointed embroiderer's scissors.

4. A thimble.

5. Fine-line Magic Marker pens in colors being used, plus a black one.

6. A packet of #18–#22 chenille needles. They have a large eye and a sharp point. Paradoxically, the smaller the number, the bigger the needle. Which to employ depends upon the bulk of the yarn being used.

7. A small container—I use a tin pastille box—to hold the odd separations of yarn strands which will accumulate as the Needlepainting progresses.

8. A pacifier. Cigarettes, chewing gum or Life Savers. Anything to ease the frustrations of unknotting a tangled stitch or threading a

needle, and so forth. That threading business still throws me from time
to time, especially when I'm using multi-strand wools, but I have been
able to cut down on my fumbling by using a common trick: fold your
thread over the sharp edge of the needle, where the eye is. With thumb
and index finger, tightly pull the loop against the needle until it is
flat. Slide the needle out from between the folded strand and work the
creased end of the yarn through the needle's eye. With six-strand embroidery cotton, I resort to a less genteel practice. I spit on my fingers
and pinch the end of the strand into a nice, tight, eye-poking point.

NEEDLEPAINTING

STEP 1
(See plate 3)
Unless you are a grand master at jigsaw puzzles, I would strongly ad-
vise against coloring in the poppy all at once. Do it in gradual stages
to avoid mix-ups with look-alike shades.

I always fill the green areas first with my Magic Marker. Leaves
and stems provide pronounced, natural separations. And since the center
of the flower is the focal point, I also color that. In this case, purple
for the lobed stigma and black dots (because of the white linen) to
show where the tiny white stamen should be.

STEP 2
(See plate 4)
It is time to thread your needle: first with black for the chain stitches
which will outline the circumference of the flower and the important
interior shapes: division of petals, the center, everything that breaks up
the blossom into readable segments. Use two strands of six-strand embroidery cotton because this is a small design and a thin yarn is needed
to follow the wiggly appearance of the border. To achieve the latter,

31

work in the chain stitches at different angles. One goes this way, the next a little that way.

Of course, if we were outlining a bigger flower, one full strand would be used for the chain. The number of threads is always proportionate to the size of the total design. And, naturally, the outline will not always be done in black. I used it in this sample to show the effectiveness of sharp contrast. Nature is usually more subtle, and to follow her ways I usually chain-stitch with cotton, silk or rayon in a darker or lighter shade of the wool which is to fill the prescribed area. As you will see, I did this in outlining the small green leaf in the lower right-hand corner of the poppy.

Next, for those areas which appear as solid black, I used all six strands of yarn and satin stitches. Take pains to pack them close together.

The purple slices of the seed pod are done with six-strand embroidery cotton in a satin stitch.

The light flecks in the dark center of the poppy represent the delicate ends of the pollen-bearing stigma. They were made by using only two strands of six-strand, white embroidery cotton. The leftover four threads were stored in that little tin box. Small French knots (wind the thread around the needle twice) are used to get this pinpoint effect. Scatter them, irregularly, over the black, satin-stitched center.

To break down a strand, first cut off the length of cotton—it is also called floss—you need. Then untwist one end of the thread, separating the number of strands you want from the total of six.

The embroidery part of Step #2 is completed by filling in the green areas. In a chain stitch I outlined the small leaf, using a split-strand (three threads) of cotton of a lighter green than that which is planned for the leaf's surface. The latter area gets the dark-green, six-strand cotton. When filling in the body of the leaf, anchor the satin stitches through the middle of the chain stitch. That way only part of the border shows, giving the leaf an air of delicacy. In reality, that which I have been calling a small leaf is really just the tip of one, and the other green spot is what you see of that same large leaf through the petal separations. These areas, also, are satin-stitched.

Before moving on to Step #3, take a felt-tipped pen from your sewing basket and mark the areas which will get the first of the four different red yarns that make up the face of the poppy. This particular red is color #5 on the Yarn Color Key.

STEP 3
(See plate 5)
The initial use of red calls for six-strand cotton, embroidered in a very close satin stitch. Push the stitches up against each other, like people in a rush-hour subway line, to achieve a bulky, rich look.

The jagged effect of these red inserts was brought about by some-times deliberately stitching into the existing black yarn, at other times by pushing back the black—using the needle point as a pusher—at the spot where I started a new stitch.

Once again, let me emphasize that in Needlepainting you must not be a slave to guidelines. They are there merely to give you an idea of the whole poppy. The parts of that whole may, and will, vary with-out destroying the beauty of the total design. Nothing in nature is ever repeated—no two flowers, no two people are identical. Why should we want to change that law, when it comes to re-creating nature? Only machines turn out facsimiles. As a matter of fact, if you insist on be-ginning and ending every stitch exactly on the inked lines, your em-broidery will seem machine made.

Look carefully at the sampler and you will notice that besides working my thread into an existing yarn group (the black), I often start a stitch a little within the prescribed lines to leave space for when the time comes to put in a neighboring color (brilliant orange, #7 on the Yarn Color Key).

Getting ready for Step #4, I inked in the areas for yarns #6 and #7. Even though they are often side-by-side segments, the shades are so different I was not worried about getting confused when it came to matching with the right yarn.

STEP 4
(See plate 6)

I embroidered with the dark red (#6) first, working out from the center. A single strand of three-ply Persian wool was used in closely packed satin stitches.

Now, follow up by laying in the orange yarn (#7), a thin-strand acrylic. But this time the satin stitches are layered. After filling a specified area with one surface of yarn, I then worked in another on top of the first. You will notice that this second group of stitches is shorter than the preceding ones. That is because I anchored them, at random, into the center body—not the edge—of the first orange layer. By building up such textured irregularity in this outer area of the poppy, you are able to capture the effect of petals folding back.

With only one yarn more to go, there is no reason to ink in the last step. The white gaps are your final target. I try to capitalize on this saving in time by finishing with the color that calls for the most embroidering.

STEP 5
(See plate 7)

This is the best stage, the moment when all your efforts and frustrations begin to seem worthwhile. From now on, with each embroidered stitch, you will watch the poppy gradually come to life.

34

29.

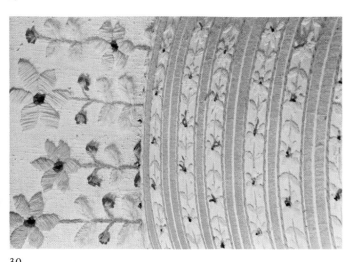

30.

29. I abhor repetition. This daisy and stripe design was executed by some patient ladies in Majorca, but . . .

30. . . . there wasn't enough fabric, so I chose an easy, nonrepeat pattern to embroider for the sofa's arm panels.

31. The same hand-embroidered, daisy fabric used in place of wallpaper and to upholster a chair.

31.

32. Moving to the reds. Poppy-appliquéd skylight shades in the solarium
protect plants, embroidery, and gros point rug from the midday sun.

33. One of a pair of Sheraton chairs to escape the white lacquer brush.
As Needlepainting softens modern, it can brighten antiques.

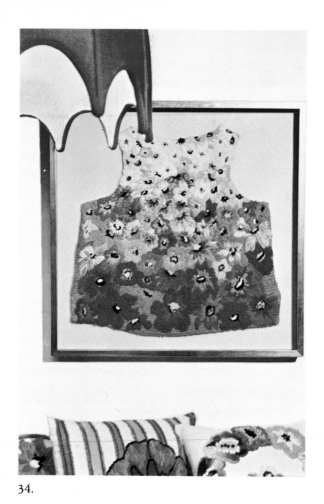

34. An embroidered tunic which had to be framed, not worn, because . . .

35. . . . after two hundred hours of stitching in yarn it weighed eight pounds.

36. I did not mind embroidering this fabric-by-the-yard design, because each flower is different.

34.

35.

36.

37.

37. Instead of using white Belgian linen, a remnant of upholstery fabric became the canvas for this Needle-painted pillow.

38. The progenitor of what was to become a long line of Oriental poppies.

39. Put out as a "wall hanging" kit, I would prefer to see it *used* on furniture or a headboard.

40. An old ice-cream-parlor chair embroidered in warm, peach blossom colors.

38.

39.

40.

41. One prescription for insomnia: a bedroom embroidered in blues,
filled with nature's peaceful gifts.

42.

43.

42. The original Corbusier lounge
was covered with black pony skin.
We, especially the dogs and cats,
prefer it this way.

43. When doing allover Needlepainting, the flowers are fitted
together like pieces in a jigsaw
puzzle.

The final yarn, the brightest red (#8), is again an acrylic, but of a thicker quality than #6 and #7. Use a satin stitch, duplicating the same layered technique started with the orange. To strengthen and accentuate the poppy's three-dimensional look, I overstitched not only twice but, here and there, three times. When you have completed your own Needlepainting, if it seems to you that certain spots need more substance, do not be afraid to add stitches over existing ones.

DO YOU LIKE IT?

The completion of any creative undertaking is a time of conflicting emotions. First there is elation, a relief that all those hours of concentrated effort have finally come to an end. Then, a vague sort of depression temporarily dampens the euphoria. It is as though your accomplishment was in the doing, not in the act of finishing. Finally, that last stitch brings on a period of anxiety. That is when embroiderers ask themselves, "Is it any good?" Too many want others to answer that query when it is really a moment of personal truth and the question ought to be, "Do I like it?"

The biggest obstacle of all to being a happily creative person is the indiscriminate desire and need to have the approval of others. This is a lovely virtue when restricted to those with whom you live, but a destructive insecurity when you want the opinion of each and every neighbor, friend and drop-in. Try pleasing all the people all the time and you end up satisfying no one—least of all yourself.

It has nothing to do with embroidery, but I think my favorite story about standing up to what-will-people-think concerns a friend of mine and the next-morning thank-you call she received. After praising his hostess's dinner menu, the caller added, "But I think I prefer your wonderful small parties to such big affairs." Ever so sweetly,

Cynthia replied, "Well, then, next time I invite you to one, don't come. That way it will be a little smaller."

If you are pleased with the outcome of your first Needlepainting, keep on going. If you have reservations about the results, do it over.

For those who are particularly satisfied with the look of a finished flower, it is nice to know that any single design can be turned into a bouquet by duplication. There are various ways to keep such a repeat from looking repetitious: First, by turning over the tracing-paper design before marking through—so that the inked outline is against the carbon paper—the flower will end up reversed on the linen. Second, the one basic pattern can be made into larger or smaller flowers by having the photostat shop blow up or reduce the design. Naturally, the different-size flowers can also be flip-flopped, as described above. Third, the original flower and subsequent variations of it may be turned clockwise or counterclockwise until their petals go in different directions. With this tracing-paper collection of design variants in front of me, I move them about, like pieces of a puzzle, until they go together in a natural-looking pattern. As the blossoms of flowers in a vase overlap, so too do some of my cutouts.

On a much larger scale, I followed this same piecing-together technique for an 11-foot by 14-foot rug. (See plate 14.) It was my first design commission upon coming to California and clearly expresses my wonderment at the profusion and richness of flowers I saw blanketing the countryside. After taking dozens and dozens of photographs of single flowers and bouquets, I cut out the parts I wanted and shuffled them around until a field of flowers emerged. My finished pattern and a sample color chart were then taken over by commercial weavers. It took them twenty months using ninety-two different shades of yarn to complete the rug. Whenever anybody complains that dedicated craftsmen no longer exist, I tell them of Stanislav V'Soske and the nearly two years he worked to make a designer's dream a reality.

36

BLOCKING

When I finished the first Thonet cover, it looked as though one of the Great Dane puppies had been teething on it. However, there was a bigger problem than that. The Needlepainting was much too small for the seat, not unlike a bikini on a size 16. I had to add, and embroider, two additional pieces of linen until the Needlepainting fit properly. Both the rumpled appearance and the shrinkage were due to my foolishly not realizing that all those stitches would pull and contract the linen. Of course, had I used a hoop none of this would have happened. But I wanted to feel the give-and-take of the backing as it absorbed each stitch.

There is another reason to explain my aversion to frames. The underside of needlework done with a hoop is uniform, neat and flat. The first two attributes are splendid, not the third. The very tangle and bunchiness of threads on the reverse side of the linen tend to increase the Needlepainting's cushiony quality. But it does not make much difference in substance. If you feel more comfortable, more secure with a hoop—use one. However, whether done on a frame or in your lap, every finished Needlepainting, like any other form of embroidery, needs blocking to some degree. Here is the method I follow:

Fill a sink with lukewarm water and a gentle soap. I use Woolite. Immerse the Needlepainting and stir it about until the suds have permeated every part of the linen and layer of yarn. Pieces which became more soiled than usual from the constant handling should be left to soak overnight. Otherwise, ten minutes should be enough. Give the embroidery a final washing in the same water, checking to see that all spots are out. Should some still remain, rub those areas with an extra helping of suds. Then, drain the sink and rinse out the Needlepainting under the cold-water tap. Finally, I rinse the piece in cold water with a quarter cup of white vinegar. It brightens the yarn colors and whitens the linen.

Almost all of today's yarns and threads are washable, but every once in a while you may have the bad luck to purchase a particular skein which was not properly treated to prevent running. To be on the safe side, before starting any Needlepainting, I take a sampling of each color yarn I plan to use and stitch them into a tiny, odd end of linen. This test strip is then soaked in hot water and soap. If none of the colors bleed, you have wasted twenty minutes; if one of the colors runs or fades, you have saved yourself countless hours of work and disappointment.

After that final vinegar rinse, hand-squeeze as much water as you can from the embroidery. Then roll it in a heavy Turkish towel to blot up the remaining moisture. Leave the embroidery in the towel while you prepare a blocking board. I have found that a piece of Celotex is best, strong enough to stand up under the tension of the stretched linen, yet sufficiently porous to let you push in tacks without bruising your thumb. All building supply stores carry Celotex in large sheets, which they will cut to your specifications. Looking ahead to future Needlepainting projects, large and small, it is wise to purchase several pieces of the board in different sizes. Also, the material can take just so many pinholes and will have to be replaced.

I wrap a clean white cloth around the board—discarded bed sheets are perfect—and tape the four ends to the back. Now, with a ruler and soft pencil, outline on the cloth the size of the linen *before* you started embroidering *plus* two inches all around. In other words, if you began with enough fabric to make a finished 14-inch by 16-inch pillow, then 16 inches by 18 inches should be the size of the rectangle you draw on the Celotex cover.

With these preliminaries out of the way, take the still damp Needlepainting from the towel and lay it out on top of the Celotex. Using the palm of your hand, push out from the center of the design toward the four corners, flattening and stretching the Needlepainting as much as possible. With aluminum push pins—get a #5 box at your local stationers; they have the longest points, five-eighths of an inch—pin down the four corners of the linen on top of the pencil-marked corners. Then follow the same tacking-down process at three or four spots along each side of the linen, always being careful to line up linen edge with penciled border.

After completing this initial staking-out process, you will notice that the Needlepainting shrank more in one direction than in the other. This is the side that should be stretched first. Therefore, turn the blocking board so that that length is perpendicular to your body. Put more tacks—they should be approximately one-half inch apart—along the border line nearest you until one edge of the linen is evenly aligned with the penciled guideline. Then, using your elbows and the underside of your arms to hold the blocking board in place, with your fingers push the embroidery outward until the far end of the linen can be tacked down along the proper mark. The process is no taffy pull. Your fingers will tire and you will expand your cursing vocabulary by 50 percent; but, half inch by half inch, you will ultimately plant another push pin, like a flag of victory. With that length put in its place, turn the blocking board ninety degrees and repeat the process in the other direction. To be sure that you are not straining the weave of the linen out of shape, constantly check that the fabric threads run parallel to each other. You can cheat a little along the edges, since the pull of the push pins makes perfect alignment impossible in these areas.

Let me hastily add that these calisthenic-type instructions need not be followed by those who embroider with a hoop. Their Needlepaintings will not have contracted to a state calling for a tug-of-war. In fact, if frame users are careful not to pull their stitches too tightly, they can do away with the blocking board altogether. A finished

Needlepainting which is only slightly disheveled may be made respectable in three easy steps: 1) Place the embroidery, face down, on a thick towel folded several times to make a soft cushion. 2) Put a damp cloth on top of the Needlepainting to eliminate any chance of scorching. 3) Using an electric iron, set at hot, push from the center of the embroidery toward the edges of the linen. That should get it back in shape and remove whatever creases were in the linen.

By the time you have finished the ironing method, the embroidery is usually dried out. Not so with the damp Needlepainting tacked to the blocking board. I usually place the latter on a terrace chair facing the sun, but when it is rainy, drizzly, foggy or smoggy in sunny Southern California, I prop the stretched embroidery near a forced-air heating vent or, in winter, in front of the living-room fireplace. Finally, I always give the blocked embroidery a good christening with spray starch.

Every so often when I have completed a Needlepainting—particularly a large one—I pamper myself by letting someone else do the blocking. Needlecraft shops and some good dry cleaners have the equipment and know-how to handle the chore. There is a charge for this service but, then, that is my present to myself. It is as soul-satisfying as having somebody in to do the dishes after a big party.

4 Color Plus White Equals Right

For many people, the biggest obstacle to a mastery of Needlepainting will not be the stitches, but the courage to use true color in their embroidery.

When one gives a small child a drawing book and a box of crayons, he or she instinctively reaches for the brightest, most exciting colors. That is true, of course, only if the child is not inhibited by a parent or a teacher.

If grown-ups would only do the same—free themselves from the blocks, fears and shyness about vibrant colors—our lives and homes would be so much happier. There is enough emotional and physical drabness in the world without compounding the gloom with dingy browns, depressing grays, hospital green and puce. (The last is such an apt name; it means "flea" color in French.)

Instead, why not counteract some of the dreariness with happy colors, a partial cure which doesn't cost a penny? They are all around us, waiting to be seen and grabbed and used—the crystal blues of sky and water, the blazing yet friendly yellow sun, the singing reds and pinks of flowers just begging to be noticed, and the rich, true greens of trees and ferns and moss. Look. They are there, and you love them. Everyone else does, too. So, there is nothing to fear.

Make it your goal to color your life as a child colors his book.

Backing down from the soapbox, let me caution that my fervent belief in colors does not mean that I advocate turning a house into a neon rainbow, where guests must wear sunglasses. Small Needlepainted areas of true color can create atmospheric brightness without gaudiness when used in conjunction with white.

Visitors entering our living room (see plate 8) frequently exclaim that they have never seen so many brilliant colors. In actual fact, except for the embroidered pieces, a tile fireplace, paintings and fresh flowers, there is very little color in that room. The walls and ceiling are dead white (it should be called "live" white), the furniture is white lacquered and there is a white shag rug on the oak floor. It is all that white which draws people's eyes to the patches of embroidered red, yellow, orange and magnifies the colors to radiant clarity.

I am not suggesting those all-white-on-white interiors which from time to time are considered the ultimate in chic, a chichi style joyously promoted by the color blind and the Cleaning Institute of America. Used in such unrelieved fashion, white is cold, monotonous and vapid. White is not meant to live alone. But as a companion for other colors, it is unbeatable. Put a pot of red geraniums on a corner table in front of a white wall and see what happens. The red flowers intensify in brilliance and the white wall becomes purer—the corner takes on a fresh vitality. Do the same thing with any other color as the background, say beige, and you will see that the plant loses its bright identity. Instead of being a cheerful focal spot, the area wilts to blandness.

The furniture in our living room became white, piece by piece, because I found that the Needlepainted cushions and seats I made for them needed a frame which highlighted the fields of stitched flowers. And the masking of wood with white achieved another effect—the furniture itself seems to blend into the walls. That is what I wanted, for with the exception of very rare and beautiful antiques, one's eye should not be made to focus on an armchair or a side table.

The same strategy to pinpoint and enhance color works in the garden. I use a row of white marguerites to backlight plantings of snapdragons, ranunculus, English primrose and calendulas. And to intensify the bold colors of my favorite Iceland poppies, I plant settings of sweet alyssum and white pansies beneath them.

Although white is the greatest setting for embroidery, it is the most frustrating background to produce because white is never *really white.* Perhaps snowflakes are before they hit the ground, but where else in nature can that elusive perfection be found? Each winter in California I plant white pansies and violets. The former are yellow-white, while the violets fool me into thinking they are close to pure white—that is, until the cyclamen are in bloom and I hold them face to face. Then the violets are shown up for what they are, dusty pretenders in need of a good scrubbing. House painters make it even harder to find the white-white I am after. Every four years, once they have covered the Needlepainted furniture with dirty drop cloths, we have the same conversation:

Head Painter, leaving cigar in mouth but turning down his portable radio: "Okay, lady, what color?"

"White."

"White?" His tone a blend of shock and real pain.

"That's right. Walls and ceiling. Just like last time."

"Okay. Ivory it is."

"No. Pure white, straight from the can."

"A touch of gray, maybe?"

"Without a touch of anything. No ocher, no gray, and *please,* no ashes."

"That kinda white is murder to paint with. Cracks are harder to cover and if you're not careful all the brush marks show."

"I know. Take a little more time."

Until the painters have left, I always have the feeling that the next phone call will be from their union saying I have been brought up on charges of gross cruelty.

Why my lifelong advocacy of and fascination with white? Perhaps it goes back to childhood. We had a martinet of a nurse who, when she wasn't sending us to bed without supper, would tell us the fairy tale of Snow White and how the princess pricked her finger embroidering. The vivid impression of that one drop of blood falling on the white linen has never left me. Sometimes, starting on a new Needlepainting, my first stitch to go through the crisp white linen will be a red one and I again hear "Hindenburg" saying, "Once upon a time . . ."

Every serious embroiderer should consider building up a personal yarn library. In the long run it is a great economy and there is never the possibility that you will be caught short in the middle of a project. Unlike needlepoint, it is impossible to know in advance precisely how much wool, silk, rayon or acrylic a yarn-hungry Needlepainting will consume. Not the least of the advantages of having your own supply on hand and in full view are the creative ideas which come from simply seeing all those skeins and balls of bright color. In addition to the supply-filled bins on my studio wall, there is a three-tiered, wire-mesh basket suspended in our bedroom, loaded with lush samplings of the colored yarns I like best. Every morning, when I am desperately searching for any legitimate reason not to get out of bed, my eyes settle on that hanging garden of possibilities. During these periods of procrastination, the lure and richness of the yarns waiting to be used have inspired a number of designs which I might otherwise never have conceived. You may call this process creativity by osmosis or plain laziness, depending upon who is lounging in bed, but it works for me. Materials do often shape the end, as the morning a shaft of sunlight came through the bedroom's French windows and haloed a cluster of golden-hued yarns. Until that moment, I had never thought of doing a sunflower design because so many had been done before. As the sun itself moved behind the skeins of fuzzy yellows, I changed my mind, got up and hurried to the studio.

Of course, pitchers and bowls of flowers around the house are an even greater source of inspiration. I pick a bouquet of the flowers I am embroidering—or buy one if the blooms are out of season—and keep it by my bedside. This way, upon waking in the morning and before turning off the light at night, I see the blossoms. Without knowing it, one becomes saturated with the hundreds of shades in every flower and attuned to the subtleties in their shapes. Then, when you sit down to Needlepaint, you subconsciously follow the colors and spirit of nature, the qualities which make them so alive. If I have a special problem getting a petal or center to look just right, the bouquet is shuttled back and forth between the bedroom and the study where I am embroidering.

I buy my yarn in needlecraft shops, department stores, supermarkets, five-and-dimes, drugstores—wherever a color or texture catches my eye. And I am just as restrictive in what I purchase: knitting wool, baby yarn, mohair and super mohair, rug yarn, angora, afghan, embroidery cottons, metallic threads, twisted cotton, acrylic, linen and rayon threads, hard twist, soft twist, no twist. Needlepaintings have a very unsophisticated appetite. They will eat up anything. Which can be a blessing for the embroiderer whose stock of a certain type yarn has run out. No more Persian wool on hand? Feed rug yarn until your next shopping trip. Like a book collector, when in strange cities I browse about the stalls for items to fill my library. I have infuriated my husband by carting through customs special shades of yarn from Mexico, Spain and Italy. Most of them faded under a 25-watt bulb or ran in blocking.

Only rarely will you encounter such defects in the yarns sold in this country. The best guarantee against any problems is a reliable needlecraft shop or department store. They hear all about the yarns they carry from the experience of their customers. They also know that needlework is rarely a onetime endeavor—embroiderers will keep coming back if they can depend on the quality of the merchandise. Since stores and sections of the country vary as to the brand of yarns carried, it would be unproductive to cover all the manufacturers in the list which follows. Therefore, I am only mentioning the makes of yarn which I like best, the ones whose quality can be counted on. Should your local needlework source not carry a particular brand, ask them if they have a comparable substitute. If not, look through the ads in any of the needlecraft magazines. There are a number of mail-order firms that sell these better yarns.

DMC tapestry wool yarn: Comes in about 350 different colors. Four-ply, which can be broken down to individual threads. But the tight twist—sign of a good yarn—is more difficult to split than most, so to prevent feathering (when the thread frizzles up) use short lengths in your needle. No worries about washing. One skein is approximately 8¾ yards.

DMC embroidery cottons: The most famous cotton in the world when it comes to lasting qualities. I remember my mother and grand-mother using it. Embroidered trousseau pieces, tablecloths, pillowcases, bedspreads, christening gowns, of DMC cotton were handed down from generation to generation. There was never any color loss, even though

46

washing in those days meant boiling. It has such a lovely sheen that some people mistake it for silk. It is six-ply, but can be used down to one-ply with great strength. Available in 328 varied colors.

DMC pearl cotton: A twisted cotton, not to be separated. Comes in sizes #5 and #3, the former being the finer. One skein of #3 measures 16.4 yards and can be had in 46 colors. There are 80 colors in the #5 line and a skein runs 27.3 yards. Size #8, another very fine thread, once was used solely for crocheting and so only comes in balls 95 yards long. Now, many people favor it for embroidery, as I do, and buying a ball is an economical purchase. I even use it for sewing on buttons.

Marlitt embroidery thread: A four-ply, 100 percent rayon. They have such a beautiful, brilliant color line that I am often tempted to buy a particularly luminous strand just to carry around with me to look at. Actually, if you are after a super high sheen, this thread will do the job better than silk. It is slippery as an eel to work with and I find it tangles, but I rather suspect that is because I use such long strands in my needle, trying to avoid the process of rethreading. It is a nontwisted thread and the skeins are 11½ yards long.

Bella Donna embroidery thread: Another rayon in lovely colors, with great texture and sheen. But it is a very soft, twisted thread, difficult to work with and sure to tangle up beginners. There are 24½ yards to a skein.

Pearsall silk thread: One skein of their "Filo Floss," six-strand, contains four yards. Silk is finer and so harder to work with than rayon. It will get caught on the slightest roughness on your fingers. Considering the high price of silk threads and the quantities which go into a Needle-painting, one might as well use the rayons. They are easier to work with and the effect is the same or better.

Zwicky silk thread: Like Pearsall, this is also made in France and equal in quality. It, too, is six-strand. They have truly lush, autumn colors. Nevertheless, for economy reasons, I would stick with the rayons when the color shade you are after can be duplicated in the synthetic.

Knox linen thread: A fine, shiny thread made in Scotland. Sometimes runs, so do not spot-clean but wash entire piece of embroidery. A skein is 18 yards.

Appleton crewel wool: A two-ply yarn, famous for the variations on one color. Used in tapestry work. Sometimes, you will find as many as nine different shades. The colors themselves are rather Old World, more subdued than those I normally use, but the firm is adding brighter ones to the line. Their line contains 325 colors and a skein is about 30 yards.

Paternayan Persian: A long fiber, 100 percent wool. An extremely strong yet soft yarn. The three plies can be broken down to two or one and used without any fear of feathering. No worries about fading or washing. Comes in more than 330 colors. An ounce is approximately 50 yards.

Bucilla, Columbia-Minerva and Paragon also make reputable three-ply wool yarns. The quality may not match Paternaya—fibers are shorter, which makes for fuzz; however, that is not a drawback in Needlepainting—but you will find their yarns widely distributed across the country. Furthermore, their wool is less expensive, although their color selection is not as wide.

Metallic embroidery thread: Elsa Williams cloisonné comes in gold and silver. Lurex makes gold, silver, copper and bronze thread.

Rug yarns: Paternaya puts out two types of heavy 100 percent wool, uncut: a hank of Shag holds about 85 yards; a hank of Pat contains 60 yards of a slightly thicker wool. Both can be bought by the strand, 63 inches. From the latter you can see the savings in buying by the bulk for a yarn library. The breadth and brilliance of their color line in rug wools is again tops. I use a great deal of it for Needlepainting. When I want a heavy stitch, instead of threading my needle with two or three strands of a lighter wool, I use one bulky strand of this.

48

Paragon has an acrylic yarn of rug weight which is called "Carissma." It comes in 35-yard skeins. Few people use acrylic in embroidery, which is a great mistake. It handles and washes beautifully; in fact, it takes certain colors which wool just won't hold. Most needlework shops do not stock the various acrylic brands, so I purchase mine at the knitting yarn counter in Woolworth's, J. C. Penney, Sears, etc. You will have to go to these same outlets for mohair, angora and ombré, since few needlecraft shops carry them.

Elsa Williams distributes a four-ply, 100 percent wool yarn. The color range is not sensational, but each color does come in five different shadings, which is a great help for people who have trouble working out the tonal components of an embroidered area that must be shaded. A good example is my Gypsy Shawl. (See plate 61.) The purple flower on it is done with several tones of purple, which could be selected from the Williams line. A skein of her yarn contains 40 yards.

5 A Pillow Is a Pillow Is a Yawn

If you find that you enjoy Needlepainting and would like to be good at it, then keep in training. There must be a continuity of effort. As in sports, cooking or gardening, embroidery skills come only with practice. However, I am proof that, in the beginning at least, practice does not necessarily make perfect.

On a wall, within clear view from the study couch on which I embroider, hangs a permanent reminder that enthusiasm and industry are not enough without experience. A thirty-inch gold frame holds my second Needlepainting project and my first big embroidery mistake. (See plate 34.)

Surprisingly pleased with the field of flowers cover for the living-room Thonet chaise, I decided to keep on with my Needlepainting. Only this time, I wanted to work on something a bit more personal —an embroidered top for an evening skirt. It was to be a simple, sleeve-less tunic following the same allover floral pattern I had used on the Thonet, but on a lesser scale. Starting with small white daisies and pansies at the top, the colors, along with the size of the flowers, gradually increased through the spectrums of pink and red until large, deep red poppies bordered the bottom of the tunic. To be sure the blend of colors was subtle, I used many different shades of yarn, constantly working them in and over each other. The center of each flower and some of the petals were highlighted with very tiny beads and sequins.

After two hundred hours of stitching, and a calloused thimble finger, the tunic was finished. My husband was present for the veiling. As I slipped it over my head, he said, "It's wonderful; only aren't you going to be hot in that?"

"Maybe. I'll have to save it for cold nights."

"Why don't you stand up straight?"

"I can't, it's too heavy."

"What do you mean? Where are you going?"

"To the bathroom, to weigh myself."

That lovely, simple little tunic with the thousands and thousands of stitches weighed eight pounds. The next morning the coat of mail went to the framer. You can't win them all, but to lose by overweight is rather embarrassing.

My husband's use of the adjective "wonderful," in reacting to the tunic, told me that something was wrong. Married couples develop their own special vocabulary in which words have a different meaning than the definitions found in a dictionary. This is especially true when two creative people live and work under the same roof. Bruce wants to know what I think of something he has written, and I am interested in his reaction to my latest designs. Neither of us intends to hurt the other, but we still have to be honest to be helpful; hence, the veiled and funny semantics of criticism. Over the years, I have come to recognize his special scale of praise. From bad to good, it goes something like this:

"Okay" = I've been wasting my time.

"Good" = Bad.

"Very good, *really*" = I had best do it over.

"That's just fine" = Mediocre.

"Wonderful" = He rather likes it, but . . .

"That really is sensational" = One of my better pieces of work.

"Wow" = My best design to date. That is what I wait to hear.

A pause before any of the above phrases, with the exception of "Wow," means Bruce cannot make up his mind; therefore, I automatically lower the rating one notch. There had been no pause before the "Wonderful" when he commented on the tunic, so all I had to do was figure out what the "but" stood for. I decided he was trying to say that the embroidered piece was just a bit too much. He was right.

Several years later, when I was designing a fashion collection, that session on the bathroom scale came vividly to mind. I wanted the gaiety and freshness of embroidery in the line, but this time I curbed my enthusiasm and limited the needlework to panels on vests, the yokes and cuffs of dresses, and on belt buckles. A little was better than a lot, as it almost always is, and the embroidered items in the collection had far greater visual impact than the field of flowers tunic.

I often hear people profess that they learn from the mistakes of others. They are very lucky, indeed. I cannot do it. Unless I go wrong on my own, I never know why or how the mistake was made. Had I not gone overboard on the Needlepainted dress top, the embroidered items in the fashion collection might have drowned in waves of impractical stitchery. Oscar Wilde wrote, "The only mistakes one never regrets are one's mistakes." And there is another saying, an old English proverb which picks me up when I fall on my face: "He who makes no mistakes never makes anything."

When I had completed that tunic top, I learned something else about Needlepainting: big projects should be followed by small ones. All conquests need not be of Everest proportions. One needs the rest,

52

the change of pace, the quick satisfaction. Instead of having to wait week to discover how something comes out, it is refreshing to finish an embroidered item in one, two or three sessions.

There are endless, small ways to apply the art of Needlepainting. And I do not mean by stuffing a house with embroidered pillows. Not that there is anything wrong with making one now and then. Actually, they are a perfect project for beginners—easy enough to make, pretty enough to inspire one to embroider more. But there ought to be a limit. Last Christmas, a friend of mine reported that she had received not one, not two but five hand-embroidered pillows from friends: "I finally understood how my husband feels each Christmas as he opens up another box of ties." When an embroiderer goes from pillow to pillow, her imagination has gone to sleep. Worse than that, the perpetual pillow pusher is missing half the fun and value of Needlepainting; for it is a craft which, if used with thought, can beautify one's everyday life on many levels.

Before the gasoline squeeze, each year in late November we were in the habit of driving down to Tijuana for a day of Christmas shopping. After a lunch of margaritas and Caesar salad, we walked—drifted is a better description—about the market stalls and shops looking for possible gifts. My husband called them pot days. To ease the minds of border custom inspectors, I should add that he was referring to my habit of loading the car with new, unpainted shapes in Mexican pottery. These were eventually painted with designs and colors I favored and are used to hold house plants or as flower vases. On one such trip, I tried to get Bruce to buy himself one of those colorfully embroidered peasant shirts. "Not me. It's much too loud." Instead he purchased a plain white one which hung in his closet, unworn. "It has no character." It took only four hours to turn a $3.50 cotton work shirt into a personalized compromise. To his surprise, and a little to mine, Bruce insists on wearing it at the knock of a guest. The bib, collar and cuffs were decorated with simple chain and satin stitches, using six-strand embroidery cotton.

Several years ago, I Needlepainted another shirt for my husband, but that is one which he still only wears under a sweater. The concept for the never-to-be-seen item came about because I like jewelry on men. He loathes the whole idea. I will never be accepted by the Women's Liberation Movement, for I firmly believe that we are given to more devious ways and thoughts than men. The case of Colen vs. Glitter is a case in point. What if I embroidered some chains and astrological charms on one of his sport shirts? Perhaps he would be amused and begin to think that male adornments were not so gauche after all. It was worth the try. And, so that Bruce would not feel too conspicuous in a gathering, I would make one for myself. (See plate 58.) Mine had to be different enough so that there was not the added stigma of His and Hers. When completed, I held them up for his inspection, careful not to give away the plot. Reaction? "They really are sensational." And, there was no pause up front—although a question followed the praise.

"Which one are you going to wear first?"

In spite of my defeat, maybe because of it, I've come to call those two embellished garments Love Shirts. They, too, were Needlepainted with embroidery cotton, plus a helping of angora and some metallic yarn. Both were done in chain and satin stitches; the flowers on mine have French knots for centers.

Sweaters can be dressed up in a similar fashion. Match the yarn to that of the sweater, wool on wool, acrylic atop acrylic and so on. The designs seem more natural that way and, besides, it uncomplicates the washing process. My choice of colors is usually in the same family group as that of the sweater. After all, if you buy a blue pullover because that shade is flattering, or matches a particular outfit, it does not make much sense to embroider it over with orange flowers. The bulkier the sweater, the more yarn and substance you can give your design; but, keep in mind that you are stitching into a more delicate material than linen. This sort of Needlepainting calls for a light hand. Instead of pulling the needle in and out, you lightly fold the stitches in—like making a soufflé. Using the same technique, scarves and knitted hats are natural subjects for these mini-Needlepaintings. But, "Beware the awful avalanche." Mini-projects have a way of growing and growing— and growing.

Among those kits I designed for *McCall's* in the late sixties, there was a fashion item that did that. Shawls were coming back in fashion about then, so I proposed a crocheted and embroidered one as an intriguing and practical project for needleworkers on the lookout for "something new." One second after Shana said, "Fine, go ahead," it occurred to me that I had not the faintest idea how to crochet. Furthermore, even if there had been time, I did not want to learn. It would be just one more thing to feel guilty about not doing. (I have a passion for freshly baked bread but have kept myself from learning how to make our own for exactly the same reason.) When someone asks what I wish for most, the answer is easy—more time.

A good friend became my ghost crocheter and made a V-shaped shawl over six feet in width. I wanted something big and warm, a wraparound which could be worn as an evening coat. In order that such a bulky thing not turn into a shoulder-bending, dray-horse blanket, I asked Frannie to please crochet the shawl in a very loose, mesh pattern, leaving a closely worked band along the edge. It was on this latter, solidly woven border that I would Needlepaint. When Frannie delivered the finished shawl, I remembered another thing which had slipped my mind, besides not knowing how to crochet—the two sides of a triangle, added together, are longer than the base. My original concept of dressing up a shawl with a few scattered flowers along the edge would never work. Big, bold flowers were the only solution, with a suggestion of a leafy vine in between to pull the design together.

Now *each* flower became a mini-Needlepainting. Multiply that times seven and the shawl was back in the maxi category.

The completed Gypsy Shawl, as it was called, had to be photographed for *McCall's*. I asked our favorite model, Dale Brown, to wear it. "I'd love to, Eszter, but I'm seven months pregnant."

"Believe me, Dale, no one will notice."

No one did. (See plate 61.)

In a lighter vein, literally as well as figuratively, for the past several years I have put a small amount of time into a Needlepainting plan which pays annual dividends on the 25th of December. I embroider Christmas tree ornaments. (See plate 50.) Vegetables and flowers may seem strange decorations, but, for me, they express the life and bounty around us—nature's 365 days of miraculous births. This Christmas I plan to add animals and birds to the collection. When Bruce lugs in the potted fir from the terrace and we hang all the embroidered decorations, it will truly be a tree of life.

Some of these little Needlepainted cutouts have ended up on things other than the branches of a yule tree. My niece "borrowed" an ear of corn and sewed it on her blue jeans as an extra pocket. When she came back for one tomato and a red pepper for elbow patches, I closed the vegetable stand. The smaller ones can be appliquéd on collars, French cuffs, the bottom of sweaters, any place you want a spot of color and whimsy. Sew two of the same design back to back, fill with dried flower petals and herbs, and you have made a sachet. Stuff the same with packed cotton and you have a pincushion . . . with sand, a paperweight. About six months ago, one of our cats knocked over the desk lamp in the study. By the time the accident was discovered, the bulb had burned a hole in the silk shade. I got out the box of Christmas ornaments and sewed a radish over the charred spot, until there was time to have the shade re-covered. The radish is still there. (See plate 56.)

However, it is with clothes needing repairs that I have the most Needlepainting fun. For instance, my love affair with blue jeans is not without moments of friction. There is something about kneeling, bending, stooping and stretching in the garden all day that tears at our relationship. Stains it, too. Bleach and the washing machine take care of the latter. Sometimes too well. Like the day I spilled some Clorox on one pant leg *after* it was washed. The bleach mark on the fabric looked like a poppy, so it became a blue Himalayan poppy—the rarest of that family.

Another Needlepainting subterfuge, stemming from a laundry-room blunder, involved a new pair of brown corduroy slacks. The first time they were put in the washing machine to get rid of the store-bought stiffness, they came calf to collar with a "Wash Only in Cold Water" blue shirt. This time, masking out the three or four tiny blue run marks with embroidered flowers did not work, aesthetically. The pants still looked spotted, now with oddly placed orange-colored blossoms. The patches needed a counterpoint for a harmonious design. I made two: irregular straight stitches in red and orange around each cuff and a jagged hemming stitch outlining the front button panel. At the same time, each buttonhole was strengthened with embroidery stitches—a practical trick which also produces an attractive visual accent.

For an interior assignment, I once worked out a very simple poppy-patterned fabric. It was silk-screen printed on unbleached cotton and used as a wall covering, on lamp and window shades. The fresh, clean look of the material pleased me so much I decided to have a summer shirt and shorts made from it. Unfortunately, the few yards I took to the dressmaker was the printer's sample strike-off which had not been chemically treated. After several washings, the yellows faded out. Several sessions of Needlepainting brought the faint poppies back to life, made the design readable and the outfit wearable.

Tears call for more extensive camouflage. A prized pair of black velvet evening pants began to show signs of my favoritism. The seat gave way. One doesn't find a perfectly fitting pair of slacks every day. These had to be preserved. I reinforced the area on the inside with black taffeta, then proceeded to Needlepaint two very large poppies on the outside. Perhaps camouflage is not quite the right word, since I used orange and red yarns in Day Glo brilliance. After all, if you're going to have fun, go all the way. Which was exactly Bruce's reaction when I got in the car one evening on our way to a party—I had to go all the way back to the bedroom and take them off.

Ever since coming to America, I had wanted to own an authentic wrangler's jacket. It had to be the real thing, not a prettied-up, woman's boutique version. I kept looking for a gentleman who fulfilled the following:

1. He had to be size 9, with long arms.
2. He had to own a worn and faded wrangler jacket.
3. He had to be willing to part with it.

It was the third requirement that was the hardest to fill, confirming an opinion I have always held—men are as clothes-conscious as women. Then along came Henry, a perfect size nine, owner of a beautifully distressed jacket. He soon became our dear friend, but friendship was not enough. Henry refused to part with what I wanted. Over the years, I tried rich, beguiling meals of chicken paprikas *and* chestnut puree, searching for a way to this man's heart. I never found it, but his stomach gradually came into view. Henry was no longer a size nine.

The jacket was mine.

After a few weeks of Needlepainting, no one could have any doubts about that. In more ways than one, I had put my hands upon the jacket. (See plates 59 and 60.) I placed them in different positions and then traced their outline with a soft lead pencil. The long finger-nails are wishful thinking. It seemed only natural that one of the hands should be holding a red poppy. The slogans chain-stitched across the faded denim—"Stick Out Your Neck," "Shoulder the Blame," "Waist Not—Want Not" and "Nix on Nixon"—were another way of per-sonalizing the jacket, of making a statement with fashion. I was having such a good time that when the jacket was completed, I went to work on a pair of matching jeans. Friends and strangers seem to share my en-joyment with the outfit, but not our local polling officials. While stand-ing in line to cast my ballot in the 1972 presidential election, they very politely asked me if I would mind turning up the waistband on the jacket. Times, though, have a way of changing. When I went to vote for local candidates in 1973, the same officials asked, "Where's your jacket, lady?"

Without going to such extremes, Needlepainting can be used in other ways to liven up one's wardrobe. Often, one embroidered ac-cessory can make a frequently worn dress or suit seem new again—a favorite ascot, for instance. (See plate 57.) A bouquet on the kitchen table of black-eyed Susans, feverfew and tithonia gave me the design notion. Few flowers are such a pure, vibrant orange as tithonia. Also known as Mexican sunflower, it can be made to grow wild in California. Something else which grows wild around our place, dammit, was in-cluded in the nosegay—crabgrass. To pull the diverse elements together, I had the flower and grass stems appear to be pinned in place by an ankh, the Egyptian symbol for life. The ascot itself was cut from a piece of silk organza and, once the bouquet was Needlepainted, folded over and hemmed.

I fell back on my love of wild flowers again when, in 1971, the editors of *House Beautiful* asked me to design some Needlepainting kits which the magazine's readers would want to buy. For the first one, we tried to think of a relatively easy project which would be useful around the house. I had just finished a quite simple drawing of native flowers and sprigs of wheat interwoven in the shape of a wreath. It would have made a lovely pillow design, but I was so set against starting the kit series with an "Oh, no, not another one" that I quickly proposed —before I had time to think—to use the wreath on place mats with matching napkins. *House Beautiful* went along with the suggestion and offered Field Flowers, as the kit was called, to its readers. (See plate 48.) All those with laundresses and/or the mothers of children with impeccable table manners wrote out their checks. You can imagine the number of orders that trickled in. The flower wreath died of neglect.

But it came back to life the next year in a less troublesome re-incarnation. That was when I signed a contract with a large company to design a line of E. H. Needlepainting kits. The creative director of the firm came out from New York and we spent the day in my studio going over possible designs. He saw a photograph of the *House Beautiful* Field Flowers tacked to the bulletin board and smiled. "That would sell like hot cakes."

"Not if anyone spills syrup," and I started to tell Steve what had happened or, I should say, what had not happened. He interrupted me,

"Oh, I don't mean as place mats, they went out with antimacassars. We'll make a sampler out of it. Have to think up an original saying to put in the middle, but don't you worry about that."

I didn't. I had visions of a giant computer being fed hundreds of different slogans until the machine stopped to smack its lips over a new, just right combination of words. Six months later the kit went on sale across the nation. In its center were the words: "Have a Nice Day."

Samplers, especially those containing original messages, are not my idea of a particularly challenging subject for Needlepainting. I know—from my royalty statements—that thousands upon thousands of needleworkers disagree with me. They are probably the same women who had the good sense not to send away for the place-mat kit. Anyway, I did have a strong affection for that wreath of wild flowers and wanted to use it someplace in the house. When Tiffany—the last of our three generations of beautiful Great Danes—died, I inscribed all their names in the center of the linen as a thank-you note for the many hours they kept me loving company while I walked the fields hunting flowers. The memorial, framed and matted in blue felt, hangs on a bedroom wall for both of us to see, should either fail to remember the good things in a not-very-gentle world.

There is another Needlepainting in the bedroom for which I have an equally strong emotional attachment. Like the wreath, The Happy Cross (see plate 47) bears witness to a rich and cherished part of my life: nature. In the formal sense of the word, one could never call me a religious person. However, I often think that flowers, trees, birds and animals were placed upon earth as a gift. If we take good care of this miraculous present, then man will always have a reminder of the true meaning of beauty, humility, love and hope. Waste or throw away the gift and we destroy ourselves. Those are the feelings, the convictions I hope the cross expresses. It is hard to believe, but there are some who think what I did with the symbol is sacrilegious and so no commercial kit maker has offered The Happy Cross for sale. It would not be the first time big business underestimated the public's taste and understanding. If you share my enthusiasm for the cross, turn to Chapter 7, "Please Pick the Flowers." There you will find the design and complete Needlepainting instructions.

6 Embroidery in Interior Design

One of the most pleasant rewards of Needlepainting is the way it can become a vital and complementary part of any interior design concept, whether the style of the house is contemporary or period. It warms the cold lines of modern, brightens the aged. And if a house is a mixture of both, like ours, embroidery will accomplish a third feat: blend the new and the old into a harmonious whole. Our marriage provided the ingredients to test the transforming powers of embroidery on all three levels.

My dowry consisted of modern furnishing from a New York City studio apartment. Bruce brought along eighteenth- and nineteenth-century antiques. We were married several hours before departing for California, so our initial view of how the possessions got along under one roof occurred when the transcontinental movers unloaded in the living room of our first, and present, home. It was as though we were attending a swap meet between the Antique Dealers Association and the acquisition committee of the Museum of Modern Art. Would the twain meet?

They had to.

After fourteen years of applying layers of white paint and Needle-painted stitches, one would never guess there had been a generation gap. Nor would anyone imagine the ambivalence with which I started the transformation process.

With the profound veneration I have for two of this century's greatest architect-designers, Breuer and Corbusier, it seemed insulting even to think about changing the look of their classic furniture. But chrome and beige wicker, no matter how magnificent the lines, seemed rather out of place in what might kindly be described as a country house in search of a facade. (Once, noticing a crack in the study ceiling, I asked my husband how he thought it happened—"The old girl had one too many face-lifts.") A little rationalizing eventually led to a special guilt-proof theorem:

A. Breuer and Corbusier meant their designs to be functional.

B. Since coming to California, I functioned best with warm colors and flowers.

C. Therefore, I would be violating the wishes of these two men if I *did not* cover their furniture with Needlepaintings.

That settled, I attacked the Corbusier lounge first, probably because it was still covered in its original fabric—black pony skin. (See plate 42.) We both felt like hypocrites sitting on that expanse of fur, while, at the same time, contributing money to prevent the slaughter of wild horses still roaming the West. The piece was in the master bedroom, where there is no air conditioning and where I wage a nightly battle against insomnia. Hot, bright colors were out. I wanted cool, go-to-sleep blues. Every spring our garden is full of these slumbering shades in cineraria, English primrose, pansies, violets and crocuses. Those were the flowers I transplanted—plus a few fantasy ones—to the Needlepainted cover for the lounge. I do not really know what Corbusier would have thought of shiny chrome plus flowers in his

63

favorite color; but, last year, I heard Marcel Breuer's reaction to a trellis of yellow poppies creeping across the seat and up the back of his beautiful armchairs, stationed at either end of our dining table. (See plate 24.) The Breuers had been my first, my dearest friends on coming to America; so, when Lajko telephoned to say he was in Los Angeles on a business trip and would like to come visit, I went down to fetch him immediately. Driving back from his hotel, I went through a stop sign. Lajko asked, "Didn't you see that?" and smiled. The smile was because he knew, I knew and the New Canaan Police Department had proof that Breuer was the worst driver in the state of Connecticut. Actually, I had not noticed the sign. All I was seeing were those two poppy-laden chairs waiting for us at home.

He saw them and smiled, touched one of the Needlepainted backs and sat down. With a sigh of relief, I slumped down in the other. We had a lovely visit.

I felt no such aesthetic restrictions when the time came to embroider seats and backs for the Thonet furniture in the living room. In fact, the skeleton-like quality of these bentwood pieces seemed to call for a little filling up. Wherever there was a stretch of wicker, I traced its outline and that became the perimeter for my Needlepainting design. That ground-breaking bit of embroidery, the Thonet lounge seat, set the pattern and color scheme for the first of its neighbors: the bentwood rocker (see plate 19), a bentwood side chair (see plate 21), and an Italian wicker-backed armchair (see plate 27). Then, for the more delicate pieces, like my favorite settee (see plate 17), and because I did not want the room overgrown with flowers, I started using sprigs and circular chains of open-faced Iceland poppies. (See plate 18.) The dining area adjoins the living room and was meant to have the same feeling; so, one by one, I embroidered the six armless dining chairs with poppy chains. (See plate 14.)

Armi Ratia, founder of Marimekko and one of the world's great fabric designers, knew of my fondness for odd Thonet pieces. In the attic of her summer home, outside Helsinki, she found an original armchair and had it shipped all the way from Finland as a Christmas present. In the cushion, Needlepainted with California poppies, for that sturdy yet beautifully simple chair, I tried to show my appreciation and love. (See plate 16.)

Speaking of this bentwood furniture, I ought to point out another pleasant aspect of putting your embroidery to work around the house. Whatever it touches, it makes special. I like Thonet because of its soft curves and honest simplicity; but, except for our early collector's items, they are not what we often hear called "valuable pieces." Faithful Thonet reproductions are on sale everywhere at very reasonable prices. In short, if you like the atmosphere of our living room and find it out of the ordinary, the look is one which all can afford. Inexpensive Needlepainting and free, bright colors are what made the transformation.

There is only one surface left to Needlepaint in the living room —the Victorian couch. Actually, I had wanted to leave this expanse of yellow just as it was in order to balance off the other field of flowers embroidery. But I have found that, although the couch was covered in heavy-duty nylon velvet, it needs to be cleaned twice as often as the Needlepainted pieces. Those layered stitches have a wonderful way of playing hide and seek with dust. If a leaf or petal gets stained, it looks —except on very close inspection—as though a shadow had been intentionally embroidered into the flower. The two Needlepainted pillows (see plate 53) on the yellow sofa were meant to mirror the tile design of the fireplace they faced. In searching for a different way to do these round cushions, I worked out a sort of embroidery plus quilting technique. As an indication of my *expertise,* only later did someone tell me that what I had done was called "tufting."

The day may not be far off when women, looking for a new embroidery challenge, decide to Needlepaint fabric by the yard. I do not mean buying a printed fabric which, like painting a picture by numbers, you overembroider here and there. For me, that is about as creative as needlepointers who purchase a canvas with the completed design and spend all their efforts simply stitching in the background. No, I am talking about a variation of what today's growing band of amateur weavers are doing—producing their own imaginative, personalized fabrics from start to finish. Any upholsterer will make an exact pattern of exactly how much embroidery you need to cover a particular sofa, headboard, and so forth. Given these dimensions, you are then able to lay out a repeat design on linen to follow in Needlepainting.

However, I could never practice what I am preaching. Having tried it once (see plate 36), I now have my own clear vision of hell —sitting hour after hour, day after day, embroidering the *same* flower over and over again. Work is nothing compared to the monotony of repetition. The next time a large piece of furniture called for embroidered fabric, I Needlepainted a 4-inch by 8-inch sample design of tiny yellow and white daisies. (See plates 29 and 30.) This swatch was then mailed to a group of even-tempered ladies in Majorca, cottage craftswomen with clean hands and a passion for repeating themselves. Eight months later the hand-embroidered material was back in this country. The fates got even with me, though, for having something done by proxy. The bolt of cloth arrived one yard short. The sofa's two armrest panels had to be Needlepainted in California.

My husband graciously turned his back while I had that antique sofa lacquered white. It was not my argument that lacquer would help preserve the old wood which moved him to acquiescence. I simply happened to ask the favor on my birthday. But he drew the color line when it came to the two fine Sheraton armchairs (see plate 33), and even I would not have dared deface the Provençal chair (see plate 44) in the blue bedroom. On one point we had no argument—whether

66

44. A Provençal chair stands among the English primroses that
inspired the colors used in the flower-strewn seat.

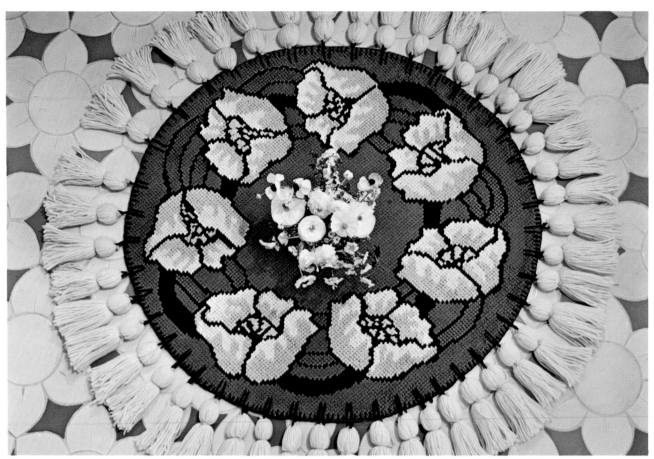

45.

45. One design can serve many mediums. This is a gros point version of the square, yellow poppy rug which was hooked.

46. A pillow of blue primroses plays host to a red ladybug.

47. Of all my Needlepaintings, The Happy Cross is the closest to my heart, for it was meant to celebrate Life.

46.

47.

48.

48. A reminder of our three Great Danes and the many hours they kept me loving company while I walked the fields hunting wild flowers.

49.

50.

51.

52.

49. Cornflowers and delphiniums for babying young or old.

50. Christmas ornaments embroidered on felt and sprinkled with glitter.

51. Ping-Pong, our Himalayan cat, where he poses best.

52. What-a-Puss (*left*) vs. The Happy Cat. Pick the winner.

53. A tufted flower design overlaid with embroidered blooms.

54. The first square in what will be a sunflower quilt.

55. No two flowers are alike. A poppy with twin pistil.

56. A burnt lampshade sprouts an embroidered radish.

53.

54.

55.

56.

57.

57. An ascot, featuring the Mexican sunflower, tithonia.

58. Love Shirts—the embroidery experiment that backfired.

58.

59. The jacket that was banned from a polling booth.

60. The hands are mine, not the long fingernails.

59.

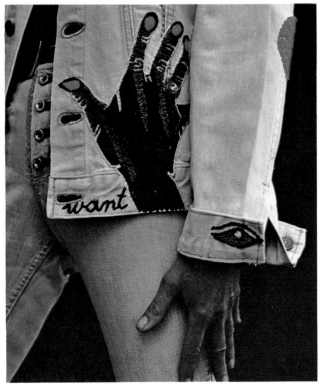

60.

61. The Gypsy Shawl.

framed in white or left in their original state, Needlepainting did seem to make the old pieces live again.

On either side of our bed there have always been two white sheepskins to lessen the shock of getting up each morning. When we were not present to say "No!", several generations of dogs and cats discovered the soothing, nap-conducive qualities of these fluffy pads. The rugs eventually looked like a pair of woebegone black sheep. There were two choices: 1) Buy two new skins and banish animals from the bedroom. Impossible. We would have to throw away all of our allergic-to-cat-hair pills and cream. And if there was no dog by the bedside, who would awaken Bruce before dawn, the silent time of day he finds best for writing? 2) Find two rugs which were more practical in color and texture. Easier said than done. Either the shades of blue were right and the rug was too delicate, or it could stand up under a herd of elephants—and came in their color.

Faced with these negatives, my resident conscience came up with a third proposal: "Why don't you make some? There must be a carload of yarn in your studio."

"I don't know how."

"What about the one on the white brick floor?"

"That's Needlepainting on felt. The Danes would ruin it in a month. We need something sturdy, like very heavy needlepoint, and that bores me."

"Then you do know how."

"Enough to be bored."

The regimentation of going in one designated hole and coming out another makes me feel like an assembly-line worker in *Modern Times.* There is none of the freedom and inventiveness of Needlepainting. Granted, this is a purely personal reaction, but what you do should be fun. If not, force yourself, and the results are usually most unhappy-looking.

I caught myself starting to sound like Betsy at day camp and decided to compromise. I would make the first bedside rug (see plate 45), but somebody else had to take over the monotonous chore of duplicating it. My aunt was to have that dubious honor.

I had not seen Lilly in over a year, although we had talked by phone. Arriving at her apartment loaded down with the recently completed rug, the painted canvas for a second one, and boxes of yarn, I immediately noticed that her arthritis had reached the crippling stage. Hands and fingers were bent to a near semicircle. She had to use two hands to turn a doorknob or to hold a glass. It was painfully obvious that asking her to thread a needle, let alone work rug-size yarn through a stiff canvas, would be a thoughtless, cruel request. However, when I left, Lilly insisted that I leave the things with her. She wanted to try at least. "Eszti, I just can't believe that my hands won't follow my heart."

For weeks after that visit, I kept brooding about what I would do if the time ever came when I could not physically make my visual dreams come true. I found no satisfactory answer until the phone rang late one evening. It was Aunt Lilly. She sounded so happy and triumphant.

"Eszti, what do you want me to do next?"

By not giving up, by fighting the stabbing pain in swollen joints, she had completed the rug. But best of all, the long hours of exercising her twisted fingers had partially cured those arthritic hands. She had regained almost half of her manual dexterity.

"My doctor can't believe it. He says I have to embroider something else right away. Make it big."

I did. A six-foot by eight-foot poppy rug for the study. (See plate 32). I worked one panel, she completed the remaining eleven. Lilly's copying was so professional that to this day I have been unable to detect which was my sample square.

I once thought it would be interesting to embroider a draft screen, one of those practical seventeenth-century panels which could be moved up or down on a brass stand and were placed next to the master's favorite wing chair to keep cool breezes from his gouty foot or arthritic shoulder. Even after fourteen years in Southern California, my husband has kept his East Coast winter reflex of sneezing at the precise moment a window is opened more than a half inch. The curtains may not rustle but his handkerchief flaps distress signals in the still room.

My idea was to Needlepaint a screen in the shape of a large poppy made up of dozens of other tiny poppies. Once again, enthusiasm got the best of good sense, and the poppy kept growing until it was a yard in diameter. Only a floor-to-ceiling pole would have been strong enough to support its weight. (See plate 23.) What do you do with a massive piece of embroidery which, mounted on a plywood backing as it was, weighed fifteen pounds? A California "happening" provided the answer. During the 1971 earthquake, one wall of our living room developed a seismograph-shaped crack of Richter scale proportions. The giant poppy became a wall hanging. A stem of woven yarn was pasted beneath the flower so that it now seems to be growing up from the chair rail.

Embroidery can be used to cover other architectural defects of a more frequent nature. The entrance to our living room was a deep, ugly doorway. It could not be remodeled or knocked out because behind the plaster of the threshold were ceiling-supporting beams. Coats of that old reliable white paint proved useless in masking the intrusive bulges. The shadows cast by them were darker than ever. I thought of running a trellis of ivy up either side of the entranceway, but there simply wasn't enough light in that area. A voice in the background was heard to say, "Embroidery doesn't need sunlight." A voice in the foreground countered with muted expletives.

I Needlepainted two stands of climbing something or others on either side of the passageway. Overhead, I continued the vine pattern until it joined a cartouche, in which nested a male and female dove, beak to beak. The idea for the latter design must have come from the warm childhood memory of being invited into a peasant's cottage. Their lives and homes were sparse, clouded by need; but over the door there was always a gay, primitive painting blessing the house and its occupants. A far more joyful and civilized custom than the "Wipe Your Feet" welcomes which greet so many of us, so often.

This climbing-vine approach to filling in a large expanse of linen with a minimum of stitchery was used once again. This time in the bedroom. King- and queen-size beds are lovely to settle down upon, but their flight-deck expanse is not very pretty to look at. Hoping to soften the look of ours, I worked out a Needepainted headboard of trellised petunias. (See plate 41.) I stitched on felt, convinced that the cats would find the fabric too soft to bother scratching. I was right. They much prefer to rub against the headboard, shedding their winter coats.

7 Please Pick the Flowers: Twenty Needlepainting Designs

Needlepainting is a progressive craft. By that I mean that you can develop creatively as slowly or as quickly as your desire, discipline and abilities allow. After practicing and gaining confidence with a commercial kit, the do-it-yourself next step is always there—if you have the courage to take it.

I have worked out the group of Needlepainting patterns which appear on the following pages. They range from rather simple to a lot of work—all are based on the designs I have used. Pick the ones you like and copy them. I hope your personal garden of stitches provides a bumper crop of happiness, satisfaction and pride.

The twenty designs can be blown up or used as is to fit your project. Perhaps you will just want to use parts of one, or you can combine the elements of several. The drawings may be transferred to canvas and used by those who enjoy needlepoint. For each pattern, there is a corresponding color photograph elsewhere in the book. Check with the latter, should you choose to use my exact color combinations or refer to a photograph in another color group. Unless indicated otherwise, all these Needlepaintings were executed on white Belgian linen.

1 BLUE ENGLISH PRIMROSE
(See plate 46)

While I did this Needlepainting in blues, English primrose comes in many different brilliant colors. Pick whichever colors please you most, but note that none of the colors is solid. They have a cast. In the case of the blue, it is purple, so to approximate that tint the chain-stitched outline of each flower was done in purple, six-strand embroidery floss.

The very center of the flower, the stigma, was encircled with small satin stitches in black embroidery floss and filled in with a light green floss, also in satin stitches. The black crisscrosses over the stigma were made by intersecting two chain stitches and tacking them down where they crossed. The orange lines running out from the center are three-strand Persian wool, split to one, in small satin stitches. The rest of this inner petal area was then completed with yellow Persian wool, three-strand, also satin-stitched. The outer parts of the petals were done in four-ply acrylic knitting yarn in satin stitches—dark blue first, followed by the light. As in all Needlepaintings, to increase the three-dimensional effect, overstitch on the outer lip of the petals.

The ladybug is satin-stitched in red and black embroidery cotton with tiny French knots for the dots. The satin-stitched leaves and stems were not outlined. The veins and part of the stems were done in greenish-yellow, Persian wool split to two strands. For the lighter green portions, use three-strand Persian.

This Needlepainting was done on a double length of linen, so that it only had to be folded over to make the front and back of the pillow case. A zipper joins the bottom edges, and, after folding back and ironing the remaining two edges, they are seamed with buttonhole stitches in a geometric pattern. If you like, finish off the pillow with two tassels made from the colored yarn most prominent in the Primrose design.

2 POPPY GARLAND
(See plate 15)

This is the design I used for our six dining chairs. It was Needle-painted on leftover pieces of upholstery fabric because I wanted different-colored backgrounds. Be sure to make copies of the design before starting, if you plan to do more than one seat. Upholstery fabric chews up the tracing. The lightest poppies went on a yellow handwoven fabric; the orange and red blossoms were worked into an orange basket weave of nylon and wool; the deepest red poppies had a very bright yellow and orange, nylon and wool background.

The embroidery work on all six chairs is identical. Flowers, petals and stems are outlined in a chain stitch of black, four-ply knitting yarn. The interior of the stems is satin-stitched with four-ply variegated green knitting yarn. The entire flower is executed in satin stitches, including the chartreuse and black centers.

Here again substance is important, so be sure to work in several layers of short and long satin stitches with doubled yarn on the outer lips of the petals to achieve a cushiony, rich feeling.

You can refer back to the color photograph for my color combinations, but one thing you should keep in mind when choosing your colors—be they greens, purple, blues or whatever your favorite—always get three shades of the same color family. This would be a good example of how the Elsa Williams shaded wool yarns can help you out, although I mixed all kinds of yarn: angora, mohair, wool and acrylic knitting yarns, all doubled or tripled for a very bold design.

3 THONET HOSTESS CHAIR
(See plate 10)

This chair represents a fuller and slightly more intricate version of the Poppy Garland.

The stems, leaves, buds, flowers and petal separations are all outlined in black, four-ply knitting wool, using chain stitches. The leaves, stems and the sheath of the buds are then filled with white angora, double strand, in satin stitches. For the flowers themselves, I used double strands of four-ply knitting wools, three-ply Persian, mohair and acrylic mixed together, in colors that started with deep burgundy, going through the shades of red, on to salmon and tones of orange and yellow and finally ending with white and black angora for the centers. With the exception of the stamen (the tiny circles on the drawing), which are mohair French knots, the entire flower and the buds are finished in lots of satin stitches packed closely together. Remember, the bigger and bolder the design, the more layers of stitches may be used. In this case, the edges of the petals call for at least three.

I can also visualize this design being greatly enlarged and transferred to canvas for a gros point rug.

4 ORNAMENTAL PATCHES
(See plates 50 and 56)

These pleasantries were originally Needleplainted on felt because that fabric had the substance I needed and does not unravel at the edges. But almost any material can be used.

Having traced the pattern on fabric, chain-stitch its circumference and important inner lines of division with any yarn you wish; just remember to keep the size of yarn and number of strands in proportion to the size of the ornament. Starting just inside the black border of each section and using a different color thread, I chain-stitched around in increasingly smaller circles until the center of that part was reached. It would have been too painstaking to do that with every kernel of corn, so each was filled with tiny satin stitches, using yellow and orange embroidery floss. For the corn husk and tassel, I went back to chain stitches in green.

Improvise on these basic designs. For instance, I wanted to imitate the bulbous edge on summer squash; therefore in that area layers of white angora were satin-stitched over the green. The same embellishing technique was followed to lay in dark shadows on the eggplant. If you are going to use the cutouts for glittering holiday ornaments, add tiny beads and rhinestones wherever it strikes your fancy. They can be pasted or sewn on. The sprig of dill weed needed such shimmering dots to highlight the tiny seeds.

You may take a mixture of these flowers and vegetables and lay them out in a circle, square or basket pattern, add some leaves, and you will end up with a design of your own. This pattern can then be Needlepainted on pillow cases, on Belgian linen for chair backs, footstools—the possibilities are as large as your inventiveness.

5 QUILTED COUCH
(See plate 36)

This particular couch cover was done on three 26-inch widths of Belgian linen. While the fabric normally comes 52 inches wide, it is easier to embroider on if the material is split.

The flowers were 3 inches in diameter and were spaced, from center to center, 4½ inches apart horizontally and 7 inches distant vertically. Of course, you can enlarge this drawing so that your flowers are bigger than mine.

I used approximately a dozen shades of red, starting with the deepest wine tones and going through the scale to the palest pink. The shapes are simple enough so that the chain-stitched border may be omitted. Every blossom contains only satin-stitched petals and centers, except for the stamen-like nubs in the middle and the black areas, which are French knots. The latter give a sense of direction and movement to the flowers, so play with this shadow effect, varying it from blossom to blossom, and you will avoid a rigid, artificial look.

This is the sort of Needlepainting in which one can use up anything and everything in the yarn library which is thick and bulky. Everything was doubled in my needle. In some instances, like with a relatively thin mohair, I quadrupled the strands. If you want more contrast, you can chain-stitch around each blossom with a slightly different color than the petals.

The border (four side panels) was Needlepainted on separate strips of linen, 6 inches wide. For the row of stylized leaves in this area, I picked out only the darker reds used in the top panel and played one tone against another in two sections of heavy satin stitches—overstitched two and three times. The black stems were made of double-strand, heavy knitting yarn in a chain stitch.

80

When the Needlepainting was completed, I had the top three sections joined together and machine-quilted in a diamond pattern. After the four sides and bottom had been added by an upholsterer, I took a large rug needle and, using two close shades of doubled knitting yarn, covered the top and bottom seams with inch-long, red chain stitches.

For those wishing to use the pattern on a large area, say a bedspread, the simplest method is to first have the design blown up to the appropriate size. Then have the blowup photostated (a relatively cheap process) as many times as is necessary to cover the piece of linen you will be embroidering. For the less ambitious, the design can be used for box pillows, chair seats, and so forth.

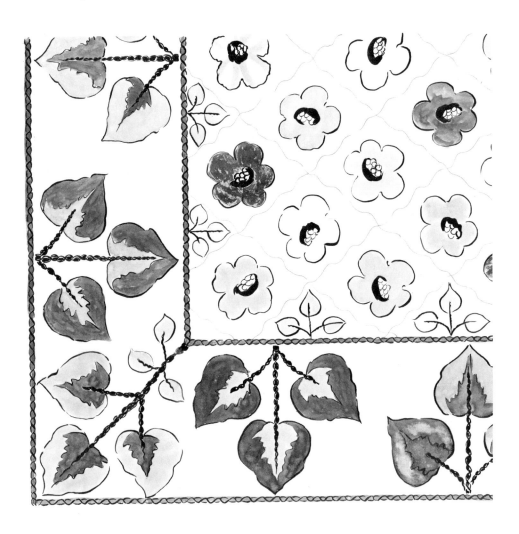

6 RED ROUND PILLOW
(See plate 37)

We needed some throw pillows to go on the quilted couch which would harmonize with that expanse of flowers yet not be lost among them. This was the solution.

On an orange and red basket-weave upholstery fabric, two circles of fanciful flowers were Needlepainted. While you will notice that the flowers are more irregular—and those in the outer circle, larger—than the blossoms atop the quilted couch, I used the same variety of yarns and colors, with the addition of a variegated red knitting wool.

The last is an easy way to achieve subtle color changes within a petal or leaf. The yarn manufacturer has graduated the tones for you. Another way to vary the color and texture is to thread your needle with two yarns that differ in type and shade, that is a shocking pink mohair with a salmon-colored wool or acrylic.

Each flower in this design was outlined in chain stitches, using the principal color of that particular blossom. Circles on the design should be filled with big, lush French knots. In the satin-stitch areas do not be afraid to sometimes work in a third or fourth layer of yarn. Those are the excesses which give this pillow its three-dimensional quality.

Of course, there is no reason why this circular pattern could not be the basis for a square pillow or seat. And just because I worked in reds does not mean you must follow suit. This, the quilted sofa and nearly all of the other designs may be done in the primary color of your choice using the different shades of that group.

7 SHERATON CHAIR SEAT
(See plate 33)

This pattern is made up of alternating wide and narrow stripes. The former are an inch wide, filled with tightly packed satin stitches of shocking pink rug yarn, for which either wool or acrylic may be picked. To the right and to the left of this satin-stitch band, I embroidered a burgundy-colored line, using three-ply wool—not doubled —in a running stitch. Right next to this strip comes a chain-stitched border of salmon pink wool, doubled in the needle. An inch and a quarter of white linen separates this stripe from the next, which is a narrow one, a half inch across. The latter is also satin-stitched, but in a slightly darker tone of pink than its neighbor. It, too, is flanked by a line of running stitches and another of chain. The colors of these remain the same, but do not double the strand in your needle when executing the chain stitch. I have been describing the layout of the stripes on our chairs, but for your own purposes, the stripes can be moved farther apart or closer together without spoiling the design.

The flower is fourteen inches in diameter at its broadest points. First outline it and the petal separations with a black chain stitch of heavy, four-ply knitting wool. The petal sections are satin stitches with deep burgundy chenille, dark red afghan, red angora and salmon mohair. All of these yarns should be doubled in the needle, and do not forget to overlay the lips of the petals generously.

The black in the center is satin-stitched with the same three-ply woolen yarn first used to outline the poppy. The white angora is also set in with satin stitches and the yellow stamens were made with French knots of three-ply wool. Finally, the green stem, which had been outlined in heavy wool chain stitches, is filled with three-ply wool in satin stitches. These must run parallel to the stitches in the pink stripes.

84

8   SHERATON CHAIR BACK

(See plate 33)

The striped background is executed in the same fashion as the seat. Just be sure that the stripes on the back will be lined up with those on the seat.

The two poppies are five, and five and one half inches in diameter. Their petals and stems were done in yarns and stitches matching those of the huge seat poppy, although the placement of color varied, and I added a light pink, three-ply wool, satin overstitch to the lips of the bottom petals in each flower. Also, instead of using white angora at the center of the blossom, the one on the left has yellow and orange three-ply wool satin-stitched between the black division lines, while the center of the right-hand poppy is filled with only orange and black. In the latter, short white running stitches, of single-ply wool, are used to suggest the stamen instead of French knots.

On this and most other Needlepainted upholstery pieces, I try to use piping made from the same colored yarns that went into the design. The larger upholstery shops have a machine that can do the twisting, or you may simply braid together three or four different yarns. If you choose to do it yourself, be sure that the piping is very tightly braided before tacking it down on top of the seams. Self-edging in this fashion helps to pull together the diverse elements of the embroidery and gives it a finished, elegant look.

9 TUFTED PILLOW
(See plate 53)

The yellow petals for this Needlepainting were cut from a woolen, basket-weave upholstery fabric. Another remnant of the same material in orange was used for the center. The dotted lines on the drawing indicate the shape of each petal and the orange cutout. Tack the seven pieces to a Belgian linen background or any other durable material which can be embroidered upon.

Now trace the design of the small flowers, marking where they fall on the orange, yellow and white areas. You will notice that the blossoms overlap all three colors. This was planned for two reasons: they help accent the shape of the design, and, when you embroider them, you will also be stitching down the appliquéd segments.

The outline of each flower is chain-stitched with single, four-ply wool knitting yarn in the color of that particular bloom. The yarns satin-stitched into the petals vary as much as the shape of the flowers. I used mohair, four-ply knitting wools, acrylics and angora—all doubled and overstitched for puffiness. The colors range from deep ocher, through the oranges and yellows, to white. Incidentally, never be afraid to Needlepaint white on white. Such areas are never lost, because it is impossible to match the background white. Also, the textured quality of the flower sets it off very effectively from the fabric surface.

The centers of the flowers, except where tiny circles on the drawing indicate French knots, were completed with satin sitches, using contrasting colors and yarns selected from the neighboring flowers. Where black accents appear in the centers, work with wool or acrylic, also in satin stitches.

After you have blocked the embroidery, turn it face down and make a short slit through the linen at the center of the petals and in

88

the middle of the orange circle. Be careful that you do not cut the yellow or orange fabrics when making these incisions. Between the linen backing and the surface fabric, insert Dacron stuffing material used in quilting. Sew up the seven slits, upholster the pillow and pipe the edge with wool yarns. Mine was made from three different shades of yellow and the tan used in Needlepainting the small flowers.

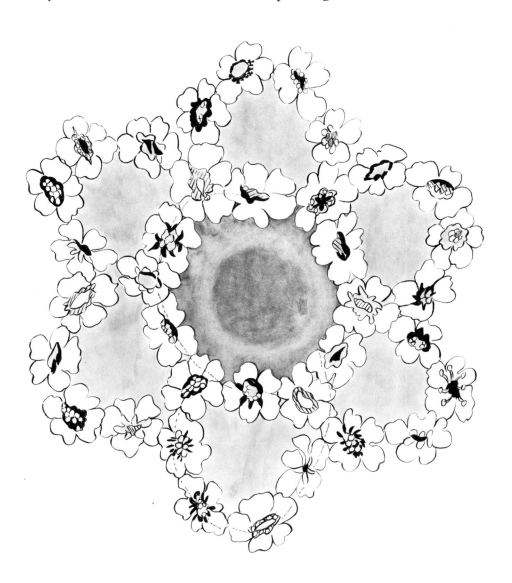

10 THONET ROCKER
(See plate 19)

When the time comes that you want to compose and execute your own allover design, keep in mind that, like an oil painting, your composition must have a focal point, one special spot which attracts the eye. In this case it is the sunflower at the lower right of the drawing. But so the design would not become top-heavy, I laid out other compensating elements, such as the yellow Iceland poppy on the left and the shaggy, make-believe blossom in red and orange at the top. Then, medium-size and small flowers were fitted in, petal to petal, with the big blossoms and with each other to get a balanced whole. Since the entire background must be covered, only portions of blossoms are placed here and there, while in other spots I had to stretch a flower out of shape in order to have it reach its neighbor—those are the ones I call fanciful.

The same irregular technique applies when you start to embroider the pattern. You play it as it comes. If certain flowers need a border to bring them into focus or to fill a gap that exists between them and the surrounding blooms, then outline with self chain stitches. If you think a particular center ought to be accentuated, then crowd in turkey knots and clip them to a convex crown. Should a flower seem lost in the crowd, overlay some satin stitches in another texture yarn or slightly brighter shade. Conversely, if a blossom looks as though it will end up claiming too much attention, substitute single-stitch stamens for the eye-catching ones in French knots. I used only satin stitches in the petals of this design, but by varying the number per flower, I was able to capture a wavy, up-and-down feeling, like a bed of flowers responding to a gentle breeze.

11 BREUER CHAIR—BACK AND SEAT

(See plates 24, 25, and 26)

What I was after here was a design device which would gap the separation between the back and the seat, allowing the two panels to flow together. Having the Iceland poppies climb a sort of trellis—of course, in nature they are not climbers—seemed to work.

The artistic-licensed trellis is embroidered in three-ply black wool or acrylic, using a chain stitch. Two such chains were laid side by side. Where you see an area on the drawing between these black lines, fill it with a single row of chain stitches in green Persian wool, split to two threads. Embroider in the stems of the buds in the same color and fashion.

The poppy in the foreground of the seat has a $6\frac{1}{4}$-inch diameter, while the remaining five flowers gradually diminish in size until the flower at the top of the back is down to about 5 inches. The same gradation takes place in color. Starting with reds on the seat, I worked my way through pinks, oranges and yellows, finally topping off the last blossom with white. Each flower and its petals were first outlined with chain stitches of four-ply knitting wool, and then the petals were loaded down with long and short satin stitches, using three-ply Persian wool, knitting yarns, mohair and angora, all doubled in the needle. The last two were worked into the lips of the petals to give them a pronounced fluffy curve. For a closer-to-nature look, you can stitch into the body of the flower, here and there, a few strands of a fourth or even fifth hue from the petals color group. The sheaths and buds were padded with satin stitches placed at a 45-degree angle.

The centers took black and white angora in satin stitches, while for the stamens I used French knots of wool.

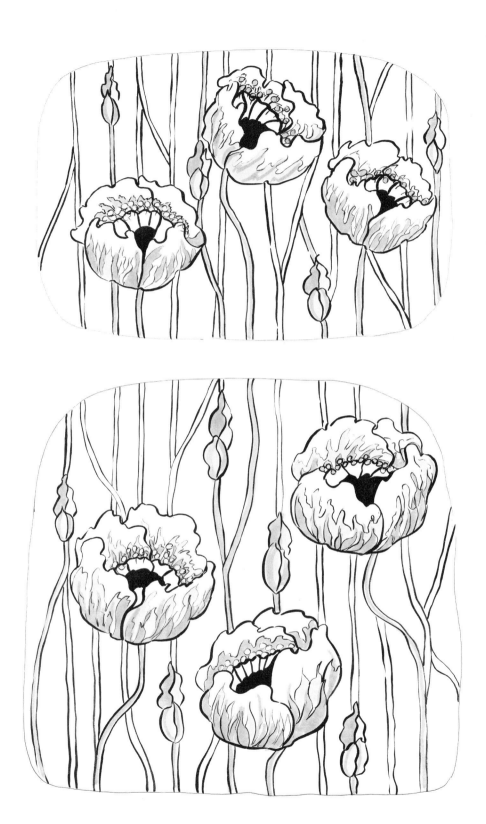

12 THONET SETTEE, SEAT
(See plate 17)

I love the graceful shape of this particular Thonet piece and tried my best to accent its beautiful lines. Once again, everything in the elongated wreath is outlined with a single row of black chain stitches. The settee was meant to accompany the Thonet hostess chair. (See page 77.) The same yarns, colors and stitches were used, starting with white angora satin stitches in the stems, leaves and sheaths of the buds and ending up with tiny buttons of French knots at the centers.

The only difference in the execution of the two pieces is that here I had a larger area to work with. Consequently, more flowers could be included in the design and I was able to make their change in color more subtle. The darkest areas at the front of the seat signify the placement of deep reds. Then, branching out to the left and right, the flowers turn orange and swing into the deeper yellows. When you get to the last three flowers, at the top of the oval, you will be working in bright yellows, overlaid with white angora.

The long, oval shape of this design suggests various other uses: the covering for a footstool or piano bench, the center motif on a bedspread, the back of a sofa, or reduced in size and Needlepainted on an oblong pillow. Last, but certainly not least, it would make a wonderful rug pattern. Should you choose to try one of these, the design works well in any color group you favor. In fact, you can even mix groups because of its progressive, melding elements.

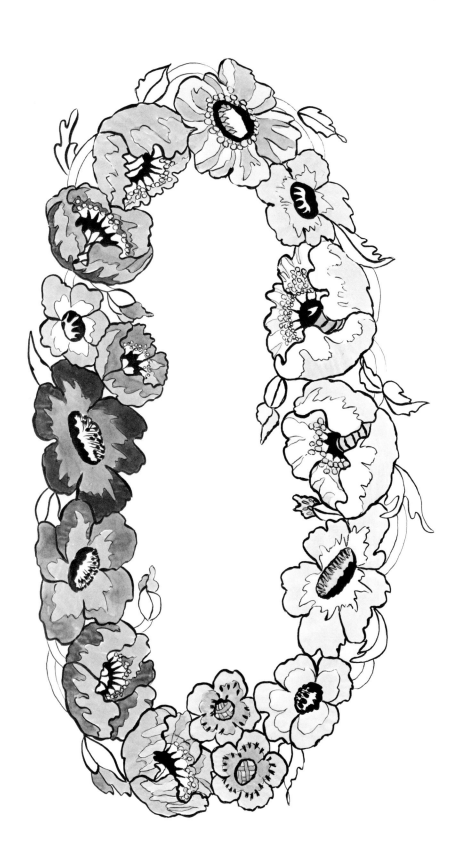

13 THONET SETTEE, BACK AND ARMS
(See plate 17)

The fan-shaped structure of the settee's back dictated this sprig-of-flowers design, with a single poppy in the center panel to serve as a visual bridge.

The drawing contains all the components needed to complete the back and arm pads. The sprig of blossoms is for the right-hand section. Flip it over to get a tracing for the left. It is made up of four Iceland poppies which vary in width from $4\frac{1}{2}$ to 5 inches. The big red poppy in the middle measures 6 inches in diameter. The miniature sprig, from base of stem to top of final red flower, is $9\frac{1}{2}$ inches.

Fill the chain-stitched borders with the same yarns and stitches used on the seat. The only difference is in the progression of colors. Instead of starting with deep reds, the bottom flower in the sprig should be a mixture of oranges with some red; the second, mostly oranges going into light tan. The third blossom contains three medium shades of yellow, while the fourth has bright yellows, with threads of white overstitched on the lips of the petals. The top flower on the arm pads roughly matches the shape and colors of the center-panel poppy.

If you are looking for other ways to use these designs consider turning over the two sprigs so that the white flowers are adjacent to each other and Needlepaint them on the back of a sofa or on a headboard. By using the design on a smaller scale, and switching from heavy wool yarns to six-strand cottons, the sprigs could be embroidered on pillowcases or sheets. The large center poppy would serve well as the nucleus of some other embroidery designs, or it can stand on its own for pillows or the backs of chairs.

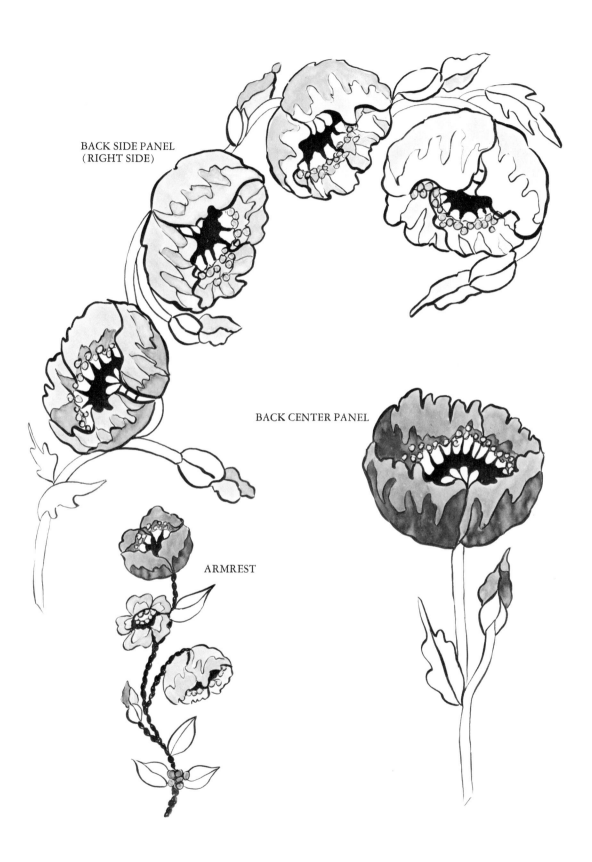

BACK SIDE PANEL
(RIGHT SIDE)

BACK CENTER PANEL

ARMREST

14 YELLOW DAISY SOFA
(See plates 29 and 30)

The drawing on the facing page contains two elements: the striped and daisy border as it appears on our sofa, minus the alternate doubled stripes, and a row of the daisies by themselves in a larger scale. If you want double stripes, it is a simple process to pair two together at whatever intervals you wish. The larger version of the daisy stripe was included for those who wished to combine a band of small flowers with a band of large ones. The Needlepainting was done on unbleached muslin, but, of course, Belgian linen can be used.

Moving from left to right, here is how the stripes actually work out on the white sofa. First, a ⅝-inch, yellow, satin-stitched band of three-ply Persian wool is flanked on either side by an orange chain-stitched line of single-ply Persian wool. Next comes a 1¾-inch band of daisies on muslin. Then, back to an orange chain line, but that is followed this time by two yellow satin-stitched stripes, a quarter inch apart—the same distance always separates chain line from satin-stitched ribbon. These last two side-by-side stripes also have a chain border a quarter inch to their right. From this point on, the placement process is simply repeated. You can group and space the stripes in any manner which suits your taste and project requirements.

Neither the leaves nor the flowers in the daisy stripe are outlined, but the stems are formed with short chain stitches of yellow Persian wool. White acrylic satin stitches were used for the flower petals, and the bright orange, black and yellow French knots in the centers are Persian wool.

The alternate, blown-up version of the daisy stripe calls for satin-stitched petals in white, black and orange satin-stitched centers, with yellow French knots as the stamens.

15 PETUNIA HEADBOARD
(See plate 41)

This design was structured so that it will fit any size bed. Adding stripes is the key to solving any discrepancy between the bed size and the wall space to be covered.

Our headboard is 70 inches by 32 inches, so I did it on blue felt which comes in 72-inch widths. It starts on the left-hand side with two single rows of navy blue chain stitches in four-ply wool. The two rows are a quarter inch apart. A half inch separates this last chain line from an inch-wide, light blue angora satin-stitched stripe. Next, three quarters of an inch away to the right is another chain-stitched line in navy blue wool. The panel is twelve and a half inches wide. The design continues in inverse order until the first panel is completed.

Running down the middle of the petunia-filled area are two four-ply navy blue wool stripes chain-stitched a half inch apart. The leaves are chain-stitched in six-strand embroidery cotton, chartreuse. They are filled with satin stitches of darker and lighter green in three-ply Persian wool. The buds and the sheaths are outlined in six-strand, black embroidery cotton, chain-stitched. These are satin-stitched with six-strand, chartreuse and white embroidery cotton. The light and dark green (same greens as the leaves) petal-like cups at the base of the flowers and the buds are outlined in black chain stitches and filled with satin stitches. The flowers, deep burgundy through the blues and purples to gray and white, are outlined in white Bella Donna chain stitches. The petals are satin-stitched in various colored, four-ply wools or acrylics. The white petals can be either four-ply wool, acrylic or angora. The centers of the petunias are filled with satin stitches, within a black chain-stitched border. The hearts of the flowers get topped off with yellow or orange French knots.

16 BABY PILLOWS
(See plate 49)

Looking carefully, you will see that the seemingly different designs on these two small pillow covers are actually composed of only three floral elements—delphinium and cornflower. On the pink one there is a sprig of each, while the blue pattern contains at its left the same delphinium, at an angle, and the same cornflower, flip-flopped in the middle. The second stalk of delphinium at the right of the blue pillow is a slight variation. The delphiniums are 11 inches in length; the cornflower is 10 inches tall on the pink pillow, but its stem was trimmed 1½ inches on the blue.

Both pillows were done entirely with six-strand embroidery cotton. At no time during the making of this design do you outline any of its leaves or flowers. The stems of the five sprigs are embroidered with tiny navy blue chain stitches, and all the leaves are satin-stitched in a light and dark shade of green. The same two greens are used in the blossom sheaths of the cornflowers. First the light green was satin-stitched into these cuplike areas. Then, single straight stitches of dark green were overembroidered in a crisscross fashion.

On the blue pillow, the delphinium on the left has three shades of purple and its center contains tiny satin stitches of orange and navy blue. The cornflower in the middle calls for two tones of blue. The remaining delphinium was done in three shades of blue, with yellow and navy blue satin stitches for the centers.

On the pink pillow, the delphinium was embroidered in red, shocking pink and light pink. The centers are navy blue and yellow. As for the cornflowers, they were done in light pink and shocking pink satin stitches.

17 BLUE PROVENÇAL CHAIR
(See plate 44)

The same Needlepainting theory and technique which governed the making of the yellow Thonet rocker seat applies to this second allover pattern.

The only difference between the two chair seats is that this one is done in blues, and in certain spots green leaves were used to fill background areas, instead of the pattern being all flowers. These leaves were first outlined and veined in dark green chain stitches of three-ply Persian wool and then satin-stitched in with a lighter green Persian yarn.

This second example of an allover pattern shows how adaptable it is to any color you wish, provided that you stay with shades and tones of that color family—plus green.

18 WHAT-A-PUSS
(See plate 52)

Here is my version of our gray Persian cat in mid-yawn, an expression which some people found "too ferocious." I wanted this finished Needlepainting of What-a-Puss to look as much like her as possible, so I clipped some of her fur and matched it up at the yarn shop. Sounds pretty ridiculous, I imagine, although I now have a very faithful portrait. I am not suggesting that you go that far, but if you do have a cat of your own and would like to use this design as the basis for its picture, match up the colors. If your favorite is a red tabby, do not embroider it What-a-Puss gray.

The cat was mostly done in long and short satin stitches, going in the direction of facial contours and expressions. If the ears point up, so should the stitches. Where wrinkles splay out from the eye, follow their line. The airy, fluffy nature of Whatta's head ruled out my enclosing it with a chain stitch. The major exception to this preponderance of satin stitches are the cheeks, which are a combination of turkey and French knots. And, the inside of the mouth plus the tip of the nose have chain stitches.

For the end of the nose, I used black and gray Persian wool. The back of the cat's throat and tongue were done in dark burgundy and strong pink Persian wool. The whiskers are twirled out with very fine chain stitches, in single-strand black Persian wool.

The white parts of the cat's face are white angora. I used four shades of gray, three-ply Persian wool which was satin-stitched in. The cat's puffy cheeks were approximated by crowding in turkey knots and pruning them long in a bubble shape. In the midst of these two bumps of yarn, work in white and black French knots. Their placement is marked on the drawing. The white teeth are done in six-strand cotton floss, satin-stitched.

106

19 GYPSY SHAWL
(See plate 61)

Obviously, the first requirement for this project is a crocheted shawl. Be sure to use a pattern that will allow you to crochet a solid band for the embroidery.

Since it is impossible to trace flower patterns onto the crochet border, cut out seven tracings of the blossom and space them out approximately a foot apart, from flower center to flower center. Pin the tracings to the wool, being sure that each flower is turned in a slightly different way. Then, using a large stitch, sew through the paper, into the shawl, along the lines which mark the three different color areas of each flower and along the line which goes around the center of each blossom. Pull off the paper and follow the same procedure with tracings of the leaves, but here only their outline need be marked with stitches.

The diagram gives the principal color of each flower, three shades of which are satin-stitched into the leaves. Don't be skimpy with the four-ply knitting yarn used for these stitches. Always thread your needle double and layer the stitches shamelessly. On such a big background, the flowers must stand out.

So that no two flowers look alike *do not* follow precisely the outside guideline which was sewn in. Extend the point of a petal or fatten a petal's sides. Internally, the flowers can be made different by varying the color and size of the huge French knots in the centers and by the judicious use of different metallic threads radiating outward along the lines of the petals. The lines running along the leaf surfaces should be approximated with running stitches of variegated green knitting yarn.

Orange

Shocking Pink

Lavender

Yellow

Magenta

Gold

Red

Trace Six Leaves of Each

Trace Two

Trace Seven

20 THE HAPPY CROSS

(See plate 47)

Only accomplished embroiderers should undertake this particular project. The design is so complicated that its satisfactory execution calls for experience in needlework. Whoever tries her hand at the cross should constantly refer to the color picture, for the work contains too many shades to identify them all. I also suggest that, for optimum understanding of the allover design, you blow up the facing drawing to the actual size of The Happy Cross, which is 16 inches wide and 22 inches tall.

With the exception of the red and blue berries, every element in this Needlepainting is self chain-stitched, using six-strand embroidery cotton split to three. The bird is outlined with white Bella Donna and filled up with concentric chain stitches—working from the outside in —of white Persian wool split to one strand. Without a separate border, the two oranges were fashioned following the same chain-stitch technique but using two plies of the wool and intermingling lighter orange accents, chain-stitched with Bella Donna. The black and chartreuse dots in the center of the berries are tiny, single French knots. Everything else on the cross is satin-stitched in a variety of yarns from angora to zinc-colored metallic thread.

The dark green holly leaves in the center of the cross were made with Bella Donna, between veins of gold metallic. Six-strand cotton was used for the leaves on the left-hand side of the cross and they also contain gold veins. The rest of the leaves, blossoms and fruits (Jerusalem cherries), are filled in with Persian wool split to two strands. The single exception to this rule was the use of white angora in the center of flowers, to accent petal lips and to capture the puffy crowns of eucalyptus buds.

110

Index

Page numbers of diagrams and pattern illustrations are indexed in italics; unpaginated color plates are indexed by plate (Pl.) number.

112